Did Christ Rule Out Women Priests

J. N. M. Wijngaards, mhm

MAYHEW-McCRIMMON
Great Wakering

PREVIOUS PUBLICATIONS by Father Wijngaards
The Formulas of the Deuteronomic Creed. Gregorian University.
Brill 1973 (Reynen, Tilburg).
*The Dramatization of Salvific History in the Deuteronomic
Schools.* Oudtestametishe Studiën Vol. XVI, Brill Lieden 1969.
Deuteronomium uit de Grondtekst Vertaald en Uitgelegd. Booken
van het Oude Testament, vol. II book 3, Romen en Zonen, Roer-
mond, 1971.
Various research articles in *Vetus Testamentum* 1965-1970, in *The
Indian Journal of Theology* 1967-1974 and in *Indian Ecclesiastical
Studies.*

First Published in Great Britain in 1977 by

MAYHEW-McCRIMMON LTD

Great Wakering Essex England

© Copyright 1977 by J. N. M. Wijngaards

ISBN 0-85597-204-1

Cover design: Neil Summerland

Printed by the printing division of

Mayhew-McCrimmon

CONTENTS

1   WHY CONTINUE THE DEBATE?   5
Conflict with the Holy Father?   7
Storm around a Scripture verse   11
The theology of slavery   14

2   WHAT DOES ROME SAY?   17
Things Rome does not say   19

3   WHY WERE MEN CONSIDERED SUPERIOR?   23
The genetic basis of sexual roles   24
Woman-centred societies   26
Domination by man   27
Social myths   29
Social myth and religion   31

4   DID CHRIST CONFORM TO SOCIAL MYTH?   33
Scrutiny of the Roman arguments   35
Jesus and the Jewish image of a 'father'   37
The roles of husband and wife in Jesus' examples   38
Jesus and Jewish biological notions   40
Women and worship   41
Conclusion: Jesus had to conform   43

5   WHAT DOES SCRIPTURE PROVE?   45
Scripture proofs for slavery   47
Recognising social myth: the dawn of light   49
Theologians come to their senses   50

6   WOULD PAUL NOT RAISE HIS EYEBROWS?   55
God thirsting for blood?   56
Wearing a veil   57
Speaking in the assembly   58
Bound up with creation?   61

7 THE IMPLICATIONS OF CHRIST'S PRIESTHOOD   63
A priesthood without 'sacred' realities   64
A priesthood in which all share   67
A priesthood of love   69

8 A VISION OF THINGS TO COME IN LUKE'S GOSPEL   73
Mary of Magdala   74
No room for the Church?   76
The Church and the Spirit   78
Ministry and the Spirit   80
Focus on women in Luke's Gospel   82
A future ministry of women   84
Our Lady's Apostolate   86
Conclusion   89

NOTES   90

1 WHY CONTINUE THE DEBATE?

Recently the Holy Father issued a statement to the effect that women cannot be ordained priests. He said the Church could never change her mind on this point as it is part of Catholic doctrine and taught by Scripture. Obviously, the Pope does not want to discriminate against women but is speaking from a sense of duty. If such is the case, why should we continue the discussion on the ministry of women and so prolong the agony?

What I mean is this: nowadays theologians are never satisfied. They will continue stirring up things regardless of what the Church may say. Surely the Holy Father knows his theology and would not make such a statement without abundant proof. The common good would be much better served if theologians would be prepared to defend rather than dispute the directives from the Holy See. What is the use of theological debate if, instead of building up the Church, it makes people disgruntled and dissatisfied?

An opinion like the above is rather off-putting. Even well-intentioned theologians — and there are some — will feel that a rug is jerked from under their feet. What is being questioned here is not the topic as such but the work of the theologian himself. He is virtually being told that there is no room for research, and that he must only defend the views forwarded by the Holy See. It is like reminding a doctor that it is his duty to *cure* not to aggravate disease.

Yet I think the opinion should be taken seriously, and that is why I am prepared to examine the fundamental question it raises.

Some theologians *have* caused confusion. A number of theological publications have indeed done more harm than good. People have a right to be annoyed at this. A theologian fulfils a public function in the Church. As such, he can be called upon to justify his actions like any other public servant.

The main question seems to be: should theologians fall in line once a statement has been issued by Rome? More specifically: are there sufficient grounds to continue the discussion on the ministry of women in spite of the Roman document of the 27th of January? In answering these questions, a lot depends on the function one ascribes to theology. If theology is supposed to do no more than give an intellectual boost to the party line, then the answer will be easy. If, however, theology is credited with the task of searching for *truth,* then the matter is not quite so easily decided.

Theology is indeed in the service of truth. It is, by definition, a reflection on revealed truth. It owes its highest allegiance to truth in whatever form this may present itself. The First Vatican Council (1869-1870) emphatically endorsed this search for truth and stated confidently that there could not be a clash between revealed truth and truth known through other channels. The reason is sound enough: God is the author of all truth and cannot contradict himself. If theology is faithful to truth, it cannot fail to be loyal to God and to his revelation.[7]

In theory this sounds fine; in practice it often leads to conflict. Or rather, in practice truth is often realised only after a fair amount of hard theological discussion. The teaching authority in the Church gives guidance in matters of doctrine and morals, but if and when this guidance does not seem to be in harmony with the truth as the theologian sees it, then there is a conflict. The theologian will then be forced in conscience to continue the search for the truth and at times he may disagree or even raise his voice in protest. This is part of the function of the theologian within the church.

It is unfortunate that theological discussion within the Church confuses people or gives them the impression that we are losing our unity of faith and fellowship. After the publication of a document such as has now appeared regarding the ministry of women, many people will look on further developments as a conflict with the Holy Father on the one side and rebellious theologians on the other. Continuing the debate may also be made to look like defiance and a refusal to submit to the official teaching authority. A book like the present one might be branded by some as a revolt against the supremacy of the Holy Father.

Such a misunderstanding must be avoided. I should like therefore to spell out in detail my role as a Catholic theologian.

The correct attitude towards statements by the Pope has been described in these words by Vatican II:

"This loyal submission of the will and intellect must be given, in a special way, to the authentic teaching authority of the Roman Pontiff, even when he does not speak *ex cathedra,* in such wise, indeed, that his supreme teaching authority be acknowledged with respect, and sincere assent be given to decisions made by him, conformably with his manifest mind and intention, which is made known principally by the character of the documents in question, or by the frequency by which a certain doctrine is proposed, or by the manner in which the doctrine is formulated." (The Church, No. 25.)[2]

To tackle the question first from a strictly legal point of view, it should be noted that the document concerning the ministry of women was a declaration published and signed by the Sacred Congregation for the doctrine of the Faith. It received papal approval in an audience granted on 15 October, 1976. According to generally accepted ecclesiastical interpretation such doctrinal declarations by the Congregation do not impede further discussion. In at least two official interpretations given, it was authoritatively stated that such documents 'have not in the least the aim to forbid that Catholic writers should study the question further and, after carefully weighing the arguments on both sides, adhere to the contrary opinion . . .' (2 June 1927); and that 'such decisions do in no way oppose the further and really scientific study of such questions' (16 January 1948). It was generally agreed, even before Vatican II, that this interpretation should be extended to all documents of the same kind and that by their very nature, these documents do not exclude further discussion.[3]

During the Vatican Council the question of free theological discussion was incorporated into the Council statements. Public opinion, with freedom of expression as a necessary constituent, plays a part in the Church: it fosters dialogue within the Church.[4] The Constitution on the Church in the Modern World speaks of such theological opinion when it states: 'All the faithful, both clerical and lay, should be accorded a lawful freedom of inquiry, freedom of thought and freedom of expression, tempered by humility and courage in whatever branch of study they have specialised.'[5] In other words the ordinary teaching authority does not rule out the freedom of expression. That this was recognised in the council itself can be illustrated by the changes in the draft (10 November 1962) which contained the following phrase, borrowed from the encyclical *Humani Generis*: 'If the Supreme Pontiffs (in the ordinary magisterium) deliberately pass judgment on a matter hitherto controversial, it should be clear to all that according to the mind and will of the Popes, the matter may not be further discussed publicly by theologians.' This sentence, however, was dropped from the final text.[6] The implication is obvious.

In their pastoral letter of 22 September 1967 the German Bishops speak at length about this problem posed by difficult statements of the ordinary magisterium. After admitting that in this ordinary magisterium 'the Church can be subject to error and has in fact erred', the Bishops affirm that, on certain conditions, individuals can disagree with the ordinary

8

magisterium and that 'in certain circumstances the faithful should have the nature and limited scope of such provisional pronouncements (of the magisterium) explained to them'. The 'certain conditions' which they stipulate were the gravity of the question, the competence to judge, and a prudent pastoral application.[7]

Having discussed some of the legal aspects (much too long, but necessary, I am afraid), I should like to dwell especially on the *spirit* of theological obedience. When the Church demands 'a loyal submission of the will and intellect' she does not ask for a renunciation of one's own power to think. The Church demands a much more valuable service, namely the honest attempt to serve the faith with all one's intellectual powers. When speaking of obedience, Vatican II envisages such a total commitment: 'They should bring their powers of intellect and will and their gifts of nature and grace to bear on the execution of commands and on the fulfilment of the tasks laid upon them.'[8] True loyalty to the truth, but also to the magisterium, requires willingness to question rather than readiness to conform. What may seem opposition at first, will eventually prove to be an active cooperation between the magisterium and the theologians towards one aim of a better formulated doctrine. Theologians play an important role in the continual reformation 'of which the Church has always a need', a reformation that also concerns 'deficiencies in the way that Church teaching has been formulated.'[9] Rather than speaking of a conflict between the magisterium and dissenting theological opinion, one should think of both as elements in a living dialogue, both equally necessary for the church's reformation.

The Pope himself sees the interplay between the teaching authority and theological study in this way. In his address to a congress of theologians on 1 October 1966 he stated: 'The magisterium draws great benefit from fervid and industrious theological study and from the cordial collaboration of the theologians. . . . Without the help of theology the magisterium could undoubtedly preserve and teach the faith, but it would

9

arrive only with difficulty at the lofty and full knowledge it needs to perform its task, since it is aware that it is not endowed with revelation or the charism of inspiration but only with the assistance of the Holy Spirit.'[10] An interesting incident of how theology and the magisterium influence one another is recorded and reflected on by G. Baum:

> 'On 11 July 1966, Pope Paul VI addressed a theological symposium meeting in Rome, on the subject of original sin. In the course of his talk, the Pope insisted that the Catholic theologian must hold that the universal sin into which man is born is a consequence of the disobedience of the single man Adam. The Catholic theologian must defend the position that all men are descendants of a single ancestor. According to press reports, the theologians present at Rome explained to Pope Paul that their meeting had studied this very question and that the available evidence hardly permitted, at this time, a categorical statement about the single ancestor Adam. When Pope Paul's talk was printed in *L'Osservatore Romano* of 15 July, significant changes had been made in the text. Instead of speaking of the single man Adam, the text simply referred to Adam, leaving room for wider interpretations of what the man Adam stands for.
>
> This is a remarkable incident for which I know no parallel. We must be grateful to the watchful theologians, the faithful servants; and we must be grateful to Pope Paul for revising his judgement after having committed himself in public. We have here the introduction of a dialogue into the exercise of magisterium. What is a little frightening about the event is its incidental character. What would have happened if they had been timid men? Theological and doctrinal issues have become so complex in our day that a single person can no longer survey the material that must be studied. . . .'.[11]

The declaration on the ministry of women is basically a document drawn up by theologians who were requested by the Holy Father to study the question. The Holy Father has lent support to their study and ordered it to be published with his approval. It merits all the respect due to such a document. If however I feel it my duty to disagree with the scriptural and theological arguments put forward in the document — and such is my conviction —, it is not with the intention of opposing the Holy Father or minimising his authority. Considering the importance of the subject matter and its great pastoral implications for the Church, I believe that a student of Scripture may not remain silent. The theological conclusions of the document seem to me totally unacceptable, and therefore harmful to the Church. I offer my view of the question in the spirit of intellectual loyalty described above.

Storm about a Scripture verse

What I have said so far will seem rather abstract and general. Those not directly familiar with theology may wonder how these principles work in practice. For such persons I thought it might be useful to relate two typical examples of how theology can be a laborious process, involving tears and blood, and dissent with prevailing theological opinion. The first example may seem trivial — it concerns only one verse from Scripture — but in fact it became a test case of theological warfare.

In 1897, the Holy Office decreed that Catholics should hold that a certain verse in the first letter of St. John (the so-called *comma ioannaeum*, 1 Jn 5, 3-5) was an authentic and inspired part of Scripture. This decree, approved by the Pope, was based on a passage in the Council of Trent which stated that 'all parts of Scripture as found in the Latin Vulgate are canonical and inspired'. The verse in question was found in the Vulgate. A doctrine proposed by a Church Council cannot be disputed. Therefore, the Holy Office argued, this verse too must be authentic and inspired.[12]

The decree was taken seriously by many 'loyal' Catholics. E. MANGENOT wrote: 'Every Catholic should submit to this disciplinary decree.' M. HETZENAUER maintained that the decree had doctrinal value; that it concerned the integrity of faith; that to doubt the authenticity of the verse in question would be the same as to 'deny that the Catholic Church is the infallible custodian and judge of the sacred books.'[13]

Scripture scholars were horrified. The disputed verse was not found in the old Greek manuscripts. It was even absent from the Latin translations until about the sixth century. One did not need to be a scholar to understand that the verse was a later addition, added to the inspired text more than five hundred years after John wrote his letter.[14] Typical of the reaction of most scholars is what A. LOISY recorded in his memoirs:

'To tell the truth, this most recent decision of the Holy Office (regarding the comma joannaem) was the most ridiculous blunder one could imagine. . . . Our scholars in France, even the anti-clerical ones among them, refrained from poking a lot of fun at the expense of the Holy Office. But people in Germany enjoyed the joke immensely and even more so in England. . . . After the blow of the bull (declaring Anglican Orders invalid) which the Archbishops of Canterbury and York had just parried by their learned reply, this next move of the Holy Office proved a beautiful chance to the Anglican theologians for taking revenge, and they did not lose time in enjoying their triumph.'[15]

Scripture scholars today are agreed that the text cannot be called authentic by any stretch of the imagination. When speaking about 'all parts of Scripture to be found in the Vulgate,' the Council of Trent did obviously not want to include such dubious later additions that could be proved to have crept into the text at a later date.

The Pope had expressed the wish that public support and mental assent should be given to such guidance of the Holy Office. Yet it is not difficult to see that no Catholic theologian worth his salt could possibly accept a decree such as that of 1897. In fact, he would fall short in his loyalty to the Church if he would not strive to point out the incongruity of the decision and to make his protest heard. Cardinal Vaughan, who happened to be in Rome at the time, was much distressed at the incident. He wrote some reassuring words to England: 'I have ascertained from an excellent source that the decree of the Holy Office on the passage of the Three Witnesses which you refer to, is not intended to close the discussion on the authenticity of that text.'[16] But this was rather meagre solace in the light of the uncompromising text of the decree itself. For many years scholars — those who had the courage to think and speak out — risked their reputation and office in an effort to point out the mistake.[17] It was only thirty years later, in 1927, that the Holy Office, with bad grace, admitted that it had been wrong.[18] No apologies were offered. No praise was given to the theologians who had contributed, at so much personal cost, to a vindication of the truth.[19]

Popes, Bishops and Councils have waged an age-long battle against many forms of heresy that threatened to deform doctrine or weaken faith. On the whole they have done a good job, witness the way in which the Church has been preserved throughout the twenty centuries of her existence. But in their anxiety to preserve, to protect, to shield and to shelter, the teachers in the Church have often been tempted to be guided by a theology that defended the *status quo*, rather than by a new creative theological quest. On the other hand the Church placed before new situations has usually been helped most by the creative insight of theologies sensitive to new demands. Hence the frequent conflict between an over-cautious, conservative theology favoured by those in authority, and a daring, dynamic theology put forward by those in the front line of pastoral involvement.

The theology of slavery

It is interesting to study the development of theology in a question such as slavery. In the feudal society of the middle ages slavery was an accepted fact. Even bishops and superiors of monasteries possessed thousands of male and female slaves employed in skilled work or in cultivating the land. In some countries the Church was the richest landowner with the greatest number of slaves. With the colonisation of the New World, the slave trade was extended to the newly-conquered lands. In his bull of 1454, *Romanus Pontifex*, Pope Nicholas V gave his blessing to the practice of enslaving conquered peoples. Slavery existed in the Papal States until the end of the 18th century and in some ecclesiastical institutions still existed as late as 1864.[20]

Slavery was a phenomenon of its own time and should be understood in its social context. But it is instructive to read how the theology of the time justified the practice with arguments taken from Scripture and Tradition. The wish to be free was interpreted as a lack of humility, as unwillingness to accept the way God had created the world. Slaves were told not to worry about their human freedom, as they should be concerned more about their spiritual life. 'We measure all human things, not with the yardstick of the body, but with that of the spirit.' It was pointed out that Jesus accepted slavery as he refers to slaves in his parables (eg Lk 12, 42 ff; 17, 7 ff), and that Paul instructed slaves to 'submit voluntarily to their masters in a spirit of humble obedience' (1 Tim 6, 1; Eph 6, 6-7; etc.).

Even great theologians like Thomas Aquinas, Albert the Great and Duns Scotus, defended slavery on theological grounds. In the seventeenth century some moralists went as far as teaching that the right of slave-ownership was a part of Catholic doctrine:

> 'It is certainly a matter of faith (*de fide*) that this sort of slavery in which a man serves his master as his slave,

is altogether lawful. This is proved from Holy Scripture, Lev 25, 39-55; 1 Pet 2, 18; 1 Cor 7, 20-24; Col 3, 11. 22; 1 Tim 6, 1-10. . . . It is also proved from reason for it is not unreasonable that just as things which are captured in a just war pass into the power and ownership of the victors, so also persons captured in war pass into the ownership of the captors. . . . All theologians are unanimous on this.'[21]

A courageous theologian such as the Dominican missionary Bartholomew de las Casas who opposed the trend of thought of his days — 'No one may be deprived of his liberty nor may any person be enslaved'[22] — was ridiculed and silenced. It was only when abolitionists had won their hardest battles for a truly egalitarian society that theology, too, came to its senses and re-examined the implications of 'the breaking down of all walls' accomplished by Christ.[23] Full ecclesiastical recognition of this came only through the Second Vatican Council, which vindicated the basic equality of all human persons and called on all 'to spare no effort to banish every vestige of social and political slavery and to safeguard basic human rights under every political system' (*Church in the Modern World*, 29).[24] Our breasts may swell at hearing this noble clarion call. It is a good thing to have it in our documents, yet I feel it is hardly a great achievement in our own day and age. Shouldn't we rather, as a Church, be proud of those rare thinkers and pastors who decried slavery on theological grounds when the common opinion and ecclesiastical thought still supported slavery? Is our best theology the one that runs after the facts and condones existing situations or the one which dares to confront established opinion with the objective demands of the Gospel?

The acceptance of slavery and the discrimination against women are closely related. In the same passage already quoted above, the Second Vatican Council states, 'Forms of social and cultural discrimination in basic personal rights on the grounds of sex, race, colour, social conditions, language or religion, must be curbed and eradicated as incompatible

15

with God's design. It is regrettable that these basic personal rights are not yet being respected everywhere, as is the case with women who are denied the chance freely to choose a husband, or state of life, or to have access to the same educational and cultural benefits as are available to men.' Excluding women from the ministry of the Church is, *prima facie*, a clear form of ecclesiastical discrimination. It is my view, shared by other Scripture scholars and theologians, that the theological reasons adduced to support the exclusion of women from the priesthood are basically an attempt to justify the *status quo* and rest on a mistaken interpretation of the New-Testament message. However disconcerting it may be to some, the discussion *must* therefore be continued until the truth in its totality is recognised and accepted.

2   WHAT DOES ROME SAY?

A good deal of publicity has been given to the Roman stand against the ministry of women, mostly adverse publicity I am sorry to say. Still, I don't have a good picture of what Rome actually did say. One picks up tidbits and snatches here and there, but I have no clear idea of the whole argument.

The Pope refuses to ordain women. That much is clear enough. But what are his reasons for adopting this view? Is it true that he says only a man can truly represent Christ? Is there a basis for this in Scripture?

My analysis of the official Roman stand will be based on a twofold document, the so-called 'Declaration on the Question of the Admission of Women to the Ministerial Priesthood,' published by the S. Congregation for the Doctrine of the Faith on Thursday 27th January 1977, and an official commentary to the text published by the Congregation on the same date.[25] To convey the contents of this document in as straightforward a manner as possible, I will re-word them in my own way, quoting key passages from the text itself in their identical words whenever possible. Here, then, is an outline of what the document contains.

All over the world women are gradually assuming their rightful place in society. In the Church, too, women are taking a more active role in various forms of the apostolate. The Church is happy about this. In the Vatican documents great stress is laid on the need of taking away all forms of discrimination against women.

Side by side with this good development, however, there is one trend that gives cause for alarm. This is the expectation now found with many that one day women too will be admitted to the ministerial priesthood. The ordination of women in Protestant Churches, and especially in Churches belonging to the Anglican communion, has helped to strengthen similar hopes in Catholic circles. Before things get out of hand, one should realise that doctrinally there is no place for women priests in the Catholic Church. This should not be understood as a form of discrimination. It is simply a factual decision in the plan of salvation that priests should be chosen from among men, not from among women.

It is true there is no explicit teaching in Scripture that restricts the priesthood only to men. How then, you may ask, can we deduce that women are excluded from the ministry? Such a conclusion can be arrived at, with practical certainty, from the combination of the following facts:

> 1. Jesus Christ chose only men to be his apostles. He obviously did this on purpose and so fixed a norm.

> 2. The Church always followed this example of Christ. Both in apostolic times and in later centuries only men have been ordained priests.

> 3. A priest is the sacramental sign of Christ's presence at the eucharist. A man can represent Christ better because Christ too was a man.

Christ counted many women among his followers, so cannot be said to have nurtured the social prejudices to which his contemporaries were subject. He could therefore easily have co-opted some women among his apostolic twelve. Choosing only men must have been a deliberate decision.

The apostles continued the same tradition. To replace Judas, 'not Mary, but Matthias was selected to be an apostle'. Although many women played leading roles in the foundation of the new christian communities among the gentiles, no woman was placed in charge of a community as its priest. Paul says that women should not speak in the church assembly (1 Cor 14, 34-35; 1 Tim 2, 12). This does not refer to a passing cultural custom such as wearing a veil on the head (Cor 11, 2-16), but seems to refer to a specific role in the Church permanently reserved to men.

Now, if it was Christ's wish that only men should be sacramental priests, the Church cannot do anything about it. The Church cannot change the substance of any sacramental sign. Christ could have chosen various substances to play a role in his sacraments. In reality, he chose water as the instrument of baptism. He chose bread and wine as the matter for the eucharistic meal. The selection of men for the priesthood must be seen as an equally specific choice of a sacramental sign. The Church cannot depart from norms laid down by Christ.

Of necessity the Incarnation took a very specific form. Theoretically speaking, God might have become flesh and lived among us as a woman. Then the whole situation would have been different. As it is, Christ was a man and therefore it is more natural that he should be sacramentally represented in the eucharist community by a man. This is also in agreement with general scriptural symbolism according to which Christ is the bridegroom and the community his bride.

'We can never ignore the fact that Christ is a man. . . . In actions which demand the character of ordination and in which Christ himself, the author of the Covenant, the Bridegroom and Head of the Church, is represented, exercising his ministry of salvation — which is in the highest degree the case in the eucharist — his role must be taken by a man. This does not stem from any personal superiority of the latter in the order of values, but only from a difference of fact on the level of functions and service.'

Things Rome does not say

The Roman document is obviously inspired by argumentation found with theologians of the traditional school. Yet it does not repeat all the traditional arguments. A process of selection has been at work. It may be worthwhile to mention briefly the two main arguments omitted in the document.

The first argument of this nature concerns the observation that God the Father is always represented as a male person in Scripture (Gen 18, 1-2; Is 6, 1-3; Dan 7, 9). The male person, it is then stated, is a better image of the Divinity on account of his masculine nature. So it is natural that men, rather than women, should be called upon to speak and act on behalf of God.

Man is superior to woman and is head of the family (Sir 25, 13-24; Eph 5, 21-23; Col 3, 18). It was God himself who subjected woman to man at creation (Gen 3, 16; Cor 11, 3; Eph 5, 23). If woman depends on man in everyday family life and secular business, how much more should she be subject to him in matters of religion.

The omission of such arguments is certainly significant. The document even goes so far as to admit prejudice against women in the theology of the past. 'It is true that in the writings of the Fathers one will find the undeniable influence of prejudices unfavourable to women.' 'The scholastic doctors, in their desire to clarify by reason the data of faith, often present arguments on this point that modern thought would have difficulty in admitting or would even rightly reject.'

Today many scholars are convinced that the selection of men for the priesthood, either by Christ, by the apostles or the church in former ages, has no doctrinal significance. It was solely due, they say, to the social status accorded to men in those times. The document however repeatedly denies the validity of this argument. 'Jesus Christ did not call women to become part of the Twelve. If he acted in this way, it was not in order to conform to the customs of his time.' Again, 'No one however has ever proved — and it is clearly impossible to prove — that this attitude (of Christ) was inspired only by social and cultural reasons.' Again, 'Social and cultural conditions did not hold back the apostles working in the Greek milieu, where the same forms of discrimination did not exist.'

It is here that we touch on the crucial issue in the debate. If we want to take the Roman document seriously — and there is no reason why we shouldn't — the exclusion of women from the priesthood is based, not on a prejudiced attitude towards the sexes, but on an historical fact (Christ excluded women) explained as a norm (women cannot be priests). The crucial question is: Is this interpretation correct? Was Christ's preference for men a practical expedient, dictated by the expectations of society in his times, or did it express a doctrinal preference which laid down a principle to be followed in all ages to come? Was the masculine character of ministers in the early Church an accident of social organisation, or was it a deliberate element of the sacramental sign? Rome says the choice of a male minister was deliberate, was doctrinal, was sacramental and normative for all times.

3 WHY WERE MEN CONSIDERED SUPERIOR?

The anti-discrimination Act has given equal opportunites to men and women. This is quite all right as far as I am concerned. Injustices have been committed in the past and it is a good thing the Government is doing something about it.

On the other hand, I feel that this equality thing is greatly exaggerated. Men and women are different. Practically all great thinkers, artists and political leaders have been men. This cannot be a coincidence. Can't we admit that man has an inborn advantage, that there is something in his make-up that gives him an edge over woman? If there are some innate qualities that make men natural leaders in society, it might explain why Christ preferred men to be his priests. Or is this argument far-fetched?

The argument is certainly not far-fetched though I would not agree with the conclusion implied in one of the last sentences. Before we can discuss the Gospel and why Christ chose men, we should first clear up this question of man's leadership role in society. Quite a lot of research has been done on this topic and the picture that has emerged is quite clear in its major outlines.[26]

The factors that have shaped the different roles of men and women in society are partly genetic, partly social. Man and woman are physically different and this predisposes them to different tasks. However, as far as leadership and domination go, these seem to have been determined mostly by the common expectations of society. It is mainly 'social myth,' through which a society lays down its own objectives and norms of behaviour, that has effectively dictated the fate of men and women.

In this chapter I will give a short survey of what various sciences have to say about the factors involved. I believe these data to be valuable as background information to our Scripture study. Readers who want to enter straight into the biblical argument, however, could skip this chapter for the time being and revert to it later, if so desired.

The genetic basis of sexual roles

Some people are so fanatic about equality of rights that they seem anxious to minimise the difference between the sexes at all costs. Unisex in clothes and trans-sexual hairstyles witness to a similar tendency. It is doubtful whether a society with more masculine women and more feminine men will be a happier community to live in. What is more, the attempt seems doomed to failure. Men and women are different, both biologically and psychologically. There are inborn traits which dispose them to different tasks in society. Although such differences should not be exaggerated, they are part and parcel of a person's physical and mental make-up. Underneath the prejudices imposed by culture, about which I will speak later, there is a hard core of constitutional variance.

Man's body is much better adapted to rough physical work. In the way man's physique is built, his central and massive body-ness is formed by the chest. Man has broad shoulders and strong arms. Man has much stronger muscles than woman, as is borne out by international sports achievements. In short, man projects an image of strength. Woman, on the other hand, possesses a body that is structured for motherhood. For her the central body-ness is constituted by the womb. 'A woman is what she is because of her womb' (Virchow). The physique of woman is 'more gracious,' obviously evolved in this way to attract the partner by its beauty and to protect the offspring by its reserves in natural energy. It stands to reason that the physical and psychological implications of motherhood dispose the woman to perform certain roles in society rather than other ones.[27]

Nor is it just a matter of physique. Men and women start life with a different emotional disposition, as has been proved by psychologists in various tests. Before boys and girls can have been influenced by prejudices of the culture to which they belong, they already show different attitudes to their environment. Generally speaking, boys play more roughly, show more aggression, are more inclined to be obstinate, are more easily given to violence. Girls yield more easily and are more affectionate. These findings have been confirmed by studies in different social milieus and cultures. Already in the first three years of life men seem to be more aggressive, women more nurturative in their approach.[28]

Confirming evidence comes from the comparative study of the behaviour of monkeys, especially that of the primates which are close to man in the pattern of evolution. Among gorillas and baboons, the males impose their authority by aggression. The leader is always a male who claims precedence over others regarding space, food and females.[29] An interesting finding is that an injection of the male sexual hormone into young females in the fetal stage produces typically male, aggressive behaviour in the young monkey.[30] This kind of research, also performed on rats, gives reason to infer that sexual hormones have a decisive influence on the behaviour of males and females.[31] The different dispositions of men and women to aggressive and nurturative tasks would seem to be related to, if not the result of, different hormone activity in the body. The massive increase of the androgen hormone in boys at puberty (from 10 to 30 times the previous level; unparalleled in girls) can demonstrably be related to the increased aggressiveness of the young adolescent.[32]

The innate differences can also be proved to some extent by the actual division of labour in society. In practically all primitive societies, aggressive jobs are done by men. It is the men who do the hunting, fishing, metal working, weapon making, boat building and so on. The women usually grind corn, gather fruit and seeds, manufacture and repair clothes, and do the work at home. Although part of this may be culture-determined, the fact that the same division of labour is followed in 224 economically primitive societies from all over the world shows that it must be partly based on the biological make-up of men and women.[33] This conclusion was recently confirmed by observations in Israel. Concerted and explicit efforts were made to give the same jobs to men and women in the kibbutz communes. In spite of this, men and women are gradually returning to an acceptance of the traditional division of labour. This is even true for the younger generation who have only experienced the practice of equal opportunities and equal work. It is again the men who work in the productive branches, while women more and more join the service branches: cooking, laundering, teaching and caring for children.[34]

Woman-centred societies

The disposition towards aggressive tasks obviously made man rather than woman a likely candidate for leadership in society. The step from aggression to dominance, however, is neither necessary nor was it universally followed. In many ancient, fruit-gathering societies it was woman, not man, who was considered the centre of the family and of tribal life. And although male dominance became the rule afterwards, some societies have preserved a matriarchal organisation to our own days.

For ancient man, the female, not the male, was the symbol of life and fertility. In the pre-agricultural phase, people did not know the biological function of the male seed. Fertility was attributed to Mother Earth, from which life was seen to spring forth in so many different forms. Undoubtedly from this fundamental experience originated the belief in the Mother Goddess. As far as we know, she is the oldest divinity worshipped by the human race. Belief in her is documented in the mythologies of Oceania, Africa, North and South America, the ancient Middle East and Asia.[35] It is supported by the paleontological finding of many female figurines, probably amulets representing the *magna mater* or fertility goddess. Some of these little statues can be dated as originating in 60,000 B.C.[36]

Among 565 societies whose social organisation was carefully studied, 20% were found to be matrilineal. In these, family membership is transmitted through the woman, not through the man. Name, heritage and descent are carried by the wife, not by the husband. Among them, 84 societies were found to be matrilocal, which means that after marriage the young couple resides with the parents of the bride, not with those of the bridegroom. Anthropologists link this social organisation to an economic situation in which the main property and source of income was the field from which women gather fruits. The centre of gravity for subsistence is fertility. It is the woman who is experienced as the social spindle round which life and daily work revolve.[37]

Domination by man

Most traditional societies that we know today show a bias towards male dominance. The supremacy of man over woman in our traditional societies is usually ascribed to economic factors. Circumstances required a more forceful form of leadership. Favoured by the genetic factors of strength and aggression, man assumed the leadership role in cattle husbandry, heavy agriculture and urbanisation. The focus on masculine power asserted itself also in religious thinking.

From about 10,000 B.C. many human societies settled down to agricultural life in small townships. We can hardly exaggerate the far-reaching consequences of this change-over. Instead of depending on what could be gathered freely or obtained by hunting, a community was forced to struggle for its existence by continuous and hard work. Man subjected animals to his use: to carry his loads and plough his lands.

Man devised tools with which he could cut materials and build lasting homes. Man fashioned weapons to meet the violence of robbers and enemies. The survival of the townships that arose depended on the strength of the workman and the valour of the soldier. It was natural that masculine power should assert itself in these new forms of society.[38]

Among the 565 primitive societies which were specially studied (mentioned above), 375 were found to be patrilocal, i.e., after marriage the family resided with the parents of the bridegroom. Also, membership in the families, with names and property rights, are transmitted through men in 4 out of every 5 societies. In all major societies known in the world at present, social organisation revolves round the man, not the woman.[39]

The new organisation of society brought with it a new vision of the world and a new understanding of God. From riveting attention on the earth and the power of birth, man began to see the world as a large city created by a Supreme Power. All the creation myths of the ancient religions that are known to us speak of a strong male god who created the world by bringing order in the chaos. Such male gods were considered to reign supreme. They were thought to rule from heaven, to display their power as warriors and supreme craftsmen. Marduk of Mesopotamia and Wodan of the Germanic tribes had the same traits. Fertility, too, was understood in a new light. It was no longer the female animal, but the male animal carrying the seed, that was considered the symbol of fertility. The bull, not the cow, came to be worshipped as the giver of life in the Middle East.[40]

The difference also manifested itself in a new attitude towards sex. Polygynism became accepted in most societies. Analysis of customs in 200 societies showed that man had appropriated many privileges regarding sex and marriage. Women, on the other hand, were subjected to severe sexual restrictions.[41] Sociologists can relate this unequal treatment of man and woman to the rise of autocratic agrarian societies.[42]

When certain values have been accepted by a society, they tend to be strengthened in the course of time by the development of a 'myth' through which these values are justified. In India, for instance, many people are convinced that the so-called castes embody higher or lower forms of human nature. The division of society into priests, warriors, merchants, farmers and outcasts is strengthened by a similar division of functions among the gods. Belief in the possibility of rebirth into higher or lower forms of life according to merit; ancient tales of superior races; superstitious preference for certain bodily traits, such as a light skin; all these confirm the acceptance of inequality. Untouchability, restricting marriage to within the caste, the observance of dietary rules peculiar to each caste and other religious customs, all form a web of convictions and practices that maintains the distinction between the different castes. The sum total of such beliefs, traditions and convictions constitutes the 'social myth' that makes the caste system possible.[43]

The acceptance of male dominance as a corner-stone of social organisation was re-inforced by a variety of forms of the same social myth.

Like the myth supporting caste, the myth of male superiority enshrines much that needs to be discarded. It springs from an outdated view of reality. It perpetuates prejudice. It proposes values no longer acceptable in a metropolitan society.

As soon as children are old enough to learn, society begins to mould their minds into its own pattern of thought. Parents impose their ideas through what they say and do. This also affects the attitude towards man or woman in society. Masculinity and femininity are two of the earliest categories assimilated by a child.[44] A study based on 110 present-day societies shows that from the fourth year of age children are pressurised into their future adult role in society. In most societies (85%), achievement and self-reliance are virtues

29

almost exclusively held out to boys. Girls are educated towards nurturance (82%) and responsibility (61%). The values thus inculcated by society become part of the myth by which man and woman judge their own characteristics and task in society.[45]

The values of a social myth can usually be recognised by the way they are expressed through language. The English language, for instance, employs the same term 'man' to denote the male person and a human being as such. By this, the male person is made the norm for human nature. Woman's nature is seen as something special, as different. It is measured against the norm of humanity found in the male. This same myth which identifies 'male' with 'being human' is also found in Sanskrit, Hebrew, Latin, Greek, French and many other languages. What some Western philosophers (Aristotle, Thomas Aquinas) have stated explicitly, 'Woman is an incomplete man'[46], is somehow the unspoken but fundamental conviction in many cultures. Although in fact woman is biologically the preserver of life and a more complete expression of human nature, she remains considered as 'the second sex, the other' (Simone de Beauvoir).

In England social myth has linked masculinity and femininity to various professions. Mathematicians, physicists and engineers are considered to exercise a 'manly' profession. They are supposed to be rough, hard, valuable, intelligent and dependable. Men novelists, poets and artists, are rated as 'feminine', with the connotation of being sexy, soft, imaginative, warm and exciting. This social rating of different professions may be one principal reason why some professions are avoided by women. Only one out of every five physicists, one of every 300 chemists, one of every 500 electrical engineers is a woman. It is not the physical work or actual ability that determines the choice, but the social conviction. Although many boys and girls have personal talents that lie in an opposite direction, they are themselves psychologically convinced they won't fit into this or that pattern because it does not agree with the social myth.[47]

Recent research on sexual behaviour in Italy disclosed unbelievable prejudices among men. In some cities 50 per cent of adult men commit adultery or have dealings with prostitutes. While excusing this as a weakness, 75 per cent of the same men will strongly condemn sexual relations of women before marriage and adultery indulged in by women. This self-contradictory attitude can be explained from a confused social myth. In popular conviction there are two kinds of women: sexless women (who should be respected) and depraved women (who may be sexually loved). An average husband in this group expects his wife to have no interest in sex (to be 'chaste' as Our Lady) and seeks sexual fulfilment with other women (whom he considers depraved like Eve). It is a mental confusion which is unhappily re-inforced by misread scriptural texts and misdirected popular devotions. For women the situation gives rise to severe psychological tensions. She cannot feel herself a true woman without having a guilt complex at the same time.[48]

It is now generally agreed that christian theology of sex, chastity, celibacy and marriage was tainted by different cultural myths in the course of the centuries. For many writers in the patristic period anything exclusively belonging to the body, and therefore irrational in stoic terms, was evil. Gregory the Great maintained that intercourse always contained an element of sin and that this element of sin consisted in the pleasure experienced.[49] Thomas Aquinas and the Scholastics based much of their theology on a cultural myth that explained marriage in terms of agriculture. The male seed was supposed to carry the complete future human being. Onanism amounted almost to abortion. In procreation, woman's contribution was considered to lie in providing a kind of human 'farm land' in which the male seed could be planted.[50]

As was stated at the end of the previous chapter, the crucial question in the debate on women priests, is whether

Christ's decision to choose his apostles only from among men was made in deference to the social myth of his time or not. If the social mentality of people in Christ's time made it practically impossible for him to appoint women as religious leaders in his Church, his choice would not rule out the ministry of women in changed times. If, however, Christ's decision was independent of such conditions, as the Vatican document maintains, and if we have then to conclude that he restricted the ministry to men on theological grounds, then his restrictive choice was meant to be a norm for all time. A dispassionate study of Scripture, which attempts to keep clear from the prejudiced explanations of former ages, should help us to decide the issue.

4 DID CHRIST CONFORM TO SOCIAL MYTH?

'Jesus Christ did not call any woman to become part of the twelve. If he acted in this way, it was not in order to conform to the customs of his time, for his attitude towards women was quite different from that of his milieu, and he deliberately and courageously broke with it.

For example, to the great astonishment of his own disciples Jesus converses publicly with the Samaritan Woman (cf. Jn 4, 27); he takes no notice of the state of legal impurity of the woman who had suffered from haemorrhages (cf. Mt 9, 20-22); he allows a sinful woman to approach him in the house of Simon the Pharisee (cf. Lk 7, 37 ff); and by pardoning the woman taken in adultery, he means to show that one must not be more severe towards the fault of a woman than towards that of a man (cf. Jn 8, 11). He does not hesitate to depart from the Mosaic Law in order to affirm the equality of the rights and duties of men and women with regard to the marriage bond (cf. Mk 10, 2-11; Mt 19, 3-9).

In his itinerant ministry Jesus was accompanied not only by the twelve but also by a group of women: 'Mary, surnamed the Magdalene, from whom seven demons had gone out, Joanna, the wife of Herod's steward Chusa, Susanna and several others who provided for them out of their own resources' (Lk 8, 2-3). Contrary to Jewish mentality, which did not accord great value to the testimony of women, as Jewish law attests, it was nevertheless women who were the first to have the privilege of seeing the risen Lord, and it was they who

*were charged by Jesus to take the first paschal message
to the apostles themselves (cf. Mt 28, 7-10; Lk 24, 9-10;
Jn 20, 11-18), in order to prepare the latter to become
the official witnesses to the resurrection. . . . It must be
recognised that we have here a number of convergent
indications that make all the more remarkable the fact
that Jesus did not entrust the apostolic charge to
women.'*

(Quotation from the Roman document on the Ministry of Women).

The Roman document is quite right in attaching great
value to the question of whether Jesus conformed to the
attitude of his contemporaries regarding women or not. As I
have stated before, this is the crucial issue in the whole
debate. If in selecting only men for the aspostolic team Jesus
was guided by the the general practice of his own times, we
have no reason to presume his objection against the ministry
of women in changed circumstances. If however Jesus broke
with the social myth of male predominance and yet refused to
admit women to the apostolic team, we have a clear indica-
tion that he was setting a permanent norm.

To proceed methodically in exposing my own view, I will
first scrutinise the Roman arguments cited above and show
that they do *not* prove Christ broke with the social customs
of his time. I will then adduce positive evidence to prove that.
Christ did conform to the social myth of male predominance
in four ways:

(a) He clung to the Jewish image of a 'father';
(b) He accepted the Jewish role of the 'husband';
(c) He spoke as if the Jewish understanding of sex was
    correct;
(d) He accommodated himself to the secondary role
    played by women in religion.

In other words, Jesus did not overthrow the social system
by which men possessed predominance in Jewish society. He
accepted this system as a social system for what it was worth
and acted in harmony with it.

The document maintains that Jesus 'deliberately and courageously broke' with the attitude towards women of his milieu. But the examples adduced do not convince. In every single case Jesus' departure from Jewish custom involved a judgment about sanctity and sin, not a judgment about the status of women. In the four cases mentioned in which Jesus showed kindness towards women: the Samaritan woman, the woman suffering from haemorrhages, the woman who washed his feet, and the woman taken in adultery, the novelty of Jesus' action lies in his compassionate behaviour towards persons supposed to be impure on account of sin. That they were women adds to the degree of his compassion but it does not change its nature. Jesus' compassion for sinful men, such as the paralytic let down through the roof, Zacchaeus, the leper at Capernaum, the good thief, etc., does not differ substantially.

Women were the first to see the empty tomb. As the document admits, it would not seem correct to speak of them as 'witnesses'. In the official list of witnesses to Jesus' resurrection of 1 Cor 15, 3-8, no woman is mentioned. The account of the empty tomb originated in all likelihood from a liturgical practice near Jerusalem.[51] Only in later times did the text assume an apologetic purpose. In harmony with Jewish thinking the apostles are then called in to function as official witnesses (Mt 28, 1-10; Jn 20, 1-10). No departure from established Jewish custom can be seen in this.

The text about divorce is interesting. The Pharisees ask, 'Is it against the law for a man to divorce his wife on any pretext whatever?'. While the rabbinical schools were divided on the gravity of the reason for which a man could divorce his wife, Jesus states that an ideal marriage should exclude the possibility of divorce. Notice how in the Jewish question itself male predominance is implied. According to Jewish law divorce was the unilateral right of the man. A husband could divorce his wife, not a wife her husband. In the Gospel of Matthew, Jesus disapproves of divorce but implicitly accepts divorce as the privilege of the husband. 'I say this to you: the man who divorces his wife, except in the case of fornication, and marries another, is guilty of adultery' (Mt 19, 9). This is probably the historical way in which Jesus answered and which would, incidentally, illustrate how Jesus conformed to the Jewish way of seeing the husband as the centre of marriage (see also Mt 5, 31-32, where again the husband is central). The formulation in Mk 10, 11-12, which also speaks of a wife divorcing her husband, is surely an explicitation, according to Jesus' mind, in the context of Mark's Roman audience.[52] According to Roman law, divorce could be initiated both by the husband and by the wife. In other words, we have here an example of Jesus' being sensitive to the rights of women; not an example of Jesus' breaking with the social myth as such.

Jesus did, of course, have a new kind of relationship with women about which I will speak at length later on (chapters 8-9). The question here is whether in these relationships with women he 'deliberately and courageously broke' with the social customs of his time. The answer is clearly: No. It is true, in one or two cases Jesus went beyond the limits which a Jewish rabbi would impose on his dealings with women. As we have seen before, this can be explained as compassion, an aspect of Jesus' overall neglect of rabbinical tradition when mercy demanded it of him (Mt 9, 12-13). There is, however, no question of a direct attack against discrimination. Jesus did not fight for the emancipation of women in the same way that he made a stand for the poor. He has frequent clashes with the pharisees about the sabbath and other traditional observances. Not once is he recorded as having a dispute to remedy the oppression woman was under. The question of emancipation simply never arose. It could not arise. The social climate was not ripe for it.

For the Jews, the man was the undisputed head of the family. All relationships centred round him. His wife and his children (especially his sons) were considered man's most precious possessions.

> 'Your wife: a fruitful vine
> on the inner walls of your house.
> Your sons: round your table,
> like shoots round an olive tree.' (Ps 128, 3)

It was the father who had absolute authority over his children and could decide about their future (Gen 43, 1-15; 2 Sam 13, 23-27). Family property was inherited by men, not by women. Only if no male heir was left, could a daughter inherit (Num 27, 1-11; 36, 1-12). It was the father who, as sole owner of the family property, could distribute it to his sons (Dt 21, 15-17). The authority of a father and the different treatment of sons and daughters in a family are well illustrated by the following piece of advice:

> 'Have you cattle? Look after them.
> If they are making you a profit, keep them.
> Have you sons? Educate them,
> make them bow the neck from childhood.
> Have you daughters? Take care of their bodies,
> but do not be over-indulgent.
> Marry a daughter off, and you have finished
> a great work;
> but give her to a man of sense.' (Sir 7, 22-25).

In New-Testament times the juridical position of man as head of the family had not changed. Jesus himself clearly presupposes it and accepts it as a fact. In the parable of the Prodigal Son (Lk 15, 11-32), it is the father who distributes the property among his sons. The willing son and the unwilling one are given their work by their father (Mt 21, 28-31). Jesus clearly presupposes the Jewish authority role of the father when he says to the pharisees; 'The devil is your father so that you do what he wants' (Jn 8, 44). Interesting in this context is also the question of Jesus' own connection to the house of David. How could Jesus be called 'Son of David' if Joseph was not his real father? Wasn't his mother Mary from the priestly tribe to which also Zechariah and Elizabeth belonged (Lk 1, 36)? The Gospels give the typically Jewish answer that, although Joseph was not the *physical* father of Jesus, he was his *legal* father as Mary's legitimate husband (Mt 1, 13-25). This would indeed convince Jews that Jesus *was* a true son of David, but it clearly implies a concept of family descent no longer valid in our own days.

In all his parables Jesus conforms to the Jewish idea according to which the man was the centre of the family. The 'owner of the house' (Lk 22, 11) is always a man. It is the man who builds the house (Mt 7, 24-27). It is the man who defends his house against intruders (Mt 12, 29) and stays awake at night to catch a burglar (Mt 24, 43). It is the man who manages the property (Mt 25, 14-30), who has authority over the servants (Mt 24, 45-51) and who controls the family store (Mt 13, 52).

The roles of husband and wife in Jesus' examples

According to Jewish thinking the wife was almost owned by her husband. He had property rights over her. 'A good wife is the best of possessions' (Sir 26, 3). 'She is far beyond the price of pearls' (Prov 31, 10). In the Ten Commandments the wife is mentioned as one of people's possessions that should be respected. 'You shall not covet your neighbour's wife, or his slave, or his maidservant, or his ox, or his donkey, or anything that is his' (Ex 20, 17). No doubt a good husband will have loved his wife and relationships between them were much more human than such juridical relationships might express. The Canticle of Canticles witnesses to this more human side of the picture. However, the ownership rights of a husband over his wife remained the juridical foundation on which the marriage bond was made. The husband could practically dissolve the bond at will (Gen 16, 1-6; Dt 24, 1-4). In extreme cases he could give her away like the Levite who, under pressure, gave his wife to the townspeople of Gibeah for their pleasure. When the poor woman died on account of the treatment she received, the townspeople were condemned for their injustice; not the Levite for giving his concubine (Judges 19, 1-30).

When speaking about marriage, Jesus takes the man-centred concept of the Jews for granted. He speaks of a *king* arranging a marriage for his son, without ever mentioning the queen (Mt 22, 1-14). At the wedding itself, it is not the bride but the bridegroom who is celebrated. The wedding guests are called 'the friends of the bridegroom' (Mt 9, 15). The ten virgins are not waiting for the bride but for the bridegroom. It is he who excludes the foolish ones from the feast (Mt 25, 1-13). It was quite natural for Jesus to say 'The bride exists only for the bridegroom' (Jn 3, 29). In passing Jesus makes mention of a man's wife and children being sold as slaves to pay off his debt (Mt 18, 25) and enumerates the wife and children among other possessions which he invites his close followers to leave for the kingdom of heaven (Lk 18, 29). Isn't it abundantly clear from all this that Jesus simply accepted the social relationships between man and woman as he found them in his own times?

The instructions of the apostles render further confirmation of this. If Jesus had rejected the social myth of man's predominance, why did they continue to strengthen it? The apostles, too, presume that the man, as father, husband and householder, wields the ultimate authority within the family. Husbands should have consideration and respect for their wives (1 Pet 3, 7). A husband should love his wife, feed her and look well after her (Eph 5, 21-33). But the wife is 'the weaker partner'. She should be obedient to her husband, faithful and conscientious (1 Pet 3, 1-7). A wife should give way to her husband (Col 3, 18), be subject to him (Eph 5, 22). Although the position of woman as an equal child of

God is recognised in some texts (Gal 3, 28), the *social* implications of this doctrine had not yet been realised.

Jesus and Jewish biological notions

The Jewish concept of male predominance was supported by a mistaken idea of sexual functions. We know that the fetus in the womb is the product of a conjunction of a male sperm and a female ovum. The Jews did not know this. They identified the fetus with the sperm. For them 'seed' and 'off-spring' are synonymous (cf Gal 3, 16). While the mother fulfilled a useful function in providing the womb, it remained the father who generated life as the carrier of 'offspring'.

Obviously, Jesus never had the intention of lecturing on the biology of sex. But when he refers to the sexual roles of man and woman in marriage, his statements conform to the Jewish notion. Neither does he correct this notion if expressed by others.

For Jesus, too, it was the man's role to produce offspring by giving his seed. The Jews argue they are offspring of Abraham because they are his direct seed, not born out of fornication (Jn 8, 39-41). Jesus accepts the custom of a man marrying his brother's widow to raise offspring for him, but denies that this type of practice will continue in heaven (Lk 20, 27-36). Jesus describes celibacy for men as 'making oneself a eunuch', a rather strong way of saying that a celibate voluntarily contains his generative power (Mt 19, 10-12). In the description of Jesus' own birth, the evangelists take the same line. Jesus is truly the Son of God because Mary did not conceive human seed, but a divine substitute for it. 'She conceived of the Holy Spirit' (Mt 1, 20). The power of the Most High overshadowed her (Lk 1, 35). In this way Jesus' own birth is the perfect example of divine sonship which John defines as being born 'not of blood nor the will of the flesh nor of the will of man, but of the will of God' (Jn 1, 13).

Woman's role is well expressed by the exclamation 'Blessed the womb that bore you and the breasts that you sucked' (Lk 11, 27). Jesus accepts this view and employs it himself when describing the future tragedy of Jerusalem when it will be said: 'Blessed are the barren, the wombs that never bore, the breasts that never gave suck' (Lk 23, 29). A woman who does not bear children is called barren: her womb is like infertile soil that cannot receive the seed. Elizabeth was called barren in this sense (Lk 1, 7. 25. 36). When discussing spiritual rebirth, Nicodemus asks: 'Does this mean that a man has to go back into his mother's womb?'. Jesus replies that, in the kingdom of heaven, man is born of 'water and the spirit'. To put it crudely, in the matrimony of baptism the Holy Spirit acts as the father engendering the seed, while the water is like the mother's womb (Jn 3, 4-8). Jesus also pre-supposes the Jewish concept of generation when describing his passion. His death is like a grain of wheat falling into the earth, dying in its womb, but being reborn with much fruit (Jn 12, 24). The anguish and labour of childbirth will be forgotten once the new child has been born (Jn 16, 21). Although such texts are by no means pronouncements, let alone inspired teaching, on the functioning of sex, they prove beyond any doubt that Jesus conformed to the views of his con-temporaries in all such matters.

Women and worship

The social myth that put man on a pedestal had enormous consequences for the way in which the Old-Testament Jew understood and practised his religion. Men and women were certainly not considered equal partners in religion or in the covenant with God. A few hard facts may help us to realise the implications of this stand.

Inequality began at birth. Whenever a child was born, the mother was considered ritually unclean for some time. If the child happened to be a boy, she was unclean for forty days; if a girl, for eighty days (Lev 12, 1-8). Every first-born male 'who opened his mother's womb' had to be redeemed with a special sacrifice. A girl did not count (Ex 13, 11-16). All male children had to be circumcised on the eighth day after birth. This was an essential condition for belonging to the Covenant, more or less parallel to our baptism for belonging to the Church. However, there was no equivalent rite of initiation for women (Gen 17, 9-14). All this was tantamount to meaning that God had concluded his covenant with the men, the 'sons of Israel'. The women participated in the Covenant only indirectly, through their fathers and husbands.

A woman could not act as a full person, independently, in her own right within religion. A religious vow made by a woman was only valid if it was ratified by her father or husband (Num 40, 2-17). Women could not present sacrifices. Their going up to the temple for worship was voluntary, not obligatory, 'Three times a year all your *menfolk* must present themselves before the Lord' (Ex 23, 17). The arrangements in the temple of Jerusalem even limited the access of women to the central sanctuary. Whereas men were allowed to proceed to the 'court of Israel' which faced the sacred precincts containing the altar of holocausts, women had to stay behind in the 'court of women'.

As in government, warfare, family life and business management, religion too was a domain where men met men. Yahweh himself was portrayed as a man. The titles under which he was invoked, King, Ruler, Warrior, Judge, Father, presented a thoroughly masculine image. The prophets could speak of him as a husband enduring the unfaithfulness of his rebellious wife, Israel (Hos 3, 1-5). Indolatry and worship of other gods was compared to fornication and adultery (Ez 16, 15-43). And although women could pray to God and at times even be his spokesmen (compare a prophetess like Deborah, Judges 4, 1-9), religion and revelation were essentially a meeting-ground between God, the Man, and his first-born son, the male Israelite. The spirit of this is well expressed in the words of God to Job:

'Gird up your loins like a man.
I will question you and you will answer me'

(Job 38, 3; 40, 7).

In this religious context, it becomes clear that a woman could never be thought of as a priest. Mosaic Law restricts the priestly ministry to Aaron and his sons (Lev 8, 1-36). The necessity of priests being men was so obvious to the Jew that in the whole Old Testament in no single text are women excluded explicitly. Whenever priests are spoken of, they are presented as men. The enormous abyss between priests and women is most clearly expressed in indirect legislation whereby a priest's 'sacredness' is safeguarded from contamination through the proximity of women. A priest should marry a virgin. He was not allowed to marry 'a woman profaned by prostitution or divorce' (Lev 21, 7-9). A priest's wife and daughters could eat from his food, including meat offered at sacrifices (Lev 22, 13). But certain of the sacrifices were sacred. Only men could eat them (Num 18, 8-10). When David and his companions were hungry and no other food was available than the 'holy bread' of the presentation sacrifice, the high-priest gave it to them reluctantly, and only after having been assured that they had not touched a woman for some days (1 Sam 21, 4-6). In this world of thought, the ministry of a woman at the altar was literally unthinkable.

Conclusion: Jesus had to conform

All these laws were in force in Jesus' time. All religious leaders — whether priests, scribes, pharisees or rabbis — were men. If this was the religious climate of the day, need we be surprised that Jesus called only men to be his apostles? To put it differently: entrusting the ministry to women would have required a profound *social* revolution, even more than a religious reform. Even if Jesus had wanted to overthrow the social structures of his society, it would be doubtful if he could have achieved this in so short a time. A centuries-old social myth that is ingrained in the texture of people's life and thought cannot be uprooted even by a God-man through three years of preaching. But Jesus did not want to effect an immediate social liberation. Although his teaching and redemptive action enshrined the principles that make true social equality possible, Jesus himself refrained from any direct social rebellion. He refused to be drawn into a political struggle for independence. He accepted discrimination against women as a reality of the society in which he lived. In selecting only men for leadership functions in his Church, Christ simply followed the social limitations forced on him by comtemporary society.

5 WHAT DOES SCRIPTURE PROVE?

In doctrinal arguments of any sort, writers will quote Scripture to prove their point. But those who hold opposing views will also quote Scripture passages or even the same ones with another interpretation. As I've heard it said, even the devil can quote Scripture. And throughout the centuries heretics have based their teachings on Scriptural texts.

In the debate whether women could be priests Scripture is quoted with equal fervour by both sides. I fail to see the use of quoting Scripture at all if its meaning can so easily be twisted. What is the use of an umpire if, at each of his decisions, the players are not clear in whose favour the decision was made? It seems to me that the debate will not make any progress until the parties agree on accepting the objective teaching of Scripture as the norm.

I am not surprised if people are sometimes exasperated by the ease with which Scripture scholars can out-quote one another. The discussion about women priests may seem to some an illustration of the same thing. One group of theologians maintains that Christ acted deliberately when he chose only men; another group maintains that he did so because of contemporary conditions. Who is right and who is wrong? I will have to go into this question, otherwise the force of my argument in the previous chapter will be lost.

It is not a waste of time to reflect a little on the *nature* of Sacred Scripture, on the kind of book it is. Contrary to a superficial impression some people have, the inspired message is rarely couched in simple and dogmatic statements. God's Word became human in its forms of expression. Teasing out the divine message from the form in which it was embedded is not always easy. But it is absolutely essential in theology. The question whether some word or deed is intentional, or only part of the frame-work, spells life or death for theological meaning. When Jesus addressed Mary as 'Woman' and added 'What have you to do with me?' (Jn 2, 4; RSV version), we have to unearth his intention from beneath the contemporary form of speaking that would seem rude to us now.

The biblical authors were inspired to teach about God and man's relationship to God. They were speaking to people of a particular culture and a particular time. Of necessity their message had to be coloured by the popular beliefs that characterised the thinking of their own contemporaries. Although the inspired message is firmly rooted in such time-bound social thought, it should not be confused with it. It would be a mistake to consider social myth, or part of it, as the message itself.

An easy example that springs to mind is the world view of the ancient Hebrews. As is well known, the earth was considered to be a flat disc with heaven, God's abode, high above it and the land of the dead in waters underneath it. The sun and the moon were looked upon as lamps that ingeniously trailed along paths across the sky. God the creator was thought of as a supreme craftsman and super-manager who called created things out of nothingness and kept them in repair by his day-to-day providence. It is now generally recognised that all this constitutes a social myth and that the details of the myth do not enter into the message itself of Scripture. God exists. He is the cause and origin of everything. This is what Scripture affirms. But *how* he created the world, whether by instant creation or through gradual evolution, is not decided by the scriptural text. Such details belong to the social myth, not the the contents of revelation.

When the question of evolution arose, it took the Church almost a century to unravel the core of inspired teaching from the Hebrew myth of creation. The reason was that scriptural texts had always been read in such a way as to blur the distinction between message and myth. One could even say that the Church *could* not see the distinction clearly before the problem had been raised. The same is true of other aspects of social myth. To illustrate how complicated this can be, I will refer to the question of slavery, touched on in chapter 1.

Scripture proofs for slavery

At first sight the Scriptural evidence justifying slavery seems overwhelming. The fundamental right of one person to own another as slave was accepted and endorsed by Hebrew law. Slaves were protected by law in certain cases (Ex 21, 2-11; 21, 26-27; Dt 23, 16-17). If the slave belonged to the Jewish people, he had the right of being liberated in a number of circumstances (Lev 25, 39-46; Ex 21, 2; Jer 34, 14). The institution of slavery itself, however, was never questioned. Before telling masters now to treat their slaves (Sir 33, 24-31), Sirach bases the inequality of free men and slaves on a disposition by God himself (Sir 33, 7-15).

From a religious point of view slaves are given some rights by way of concession. The slave or the handmaid should be given rest on the sabbath day, like the ox and the ass for that matter (Ex 20, 10; Dt 5, 14). Slaves are allowed to share in the meals concluding the peace offering (Dt 12, 18), in the paschal celebration (Ex 12, 44) and in the feasts of pentecost and tabernacles (Dt 16, 11-14).

The concept of slavery was so fundamental that it was used to characterise the relationship between God and man. Yahweh was considered the universal master, 'the Lord of lords', who owns property rights over the whole world and all men (Ps 96, 1-18; 10, 14-17). Human beings are God's slaves whose main duty it is to serve him in total obedience (Ps 123, 1-4; Is 5, 2-7; Sir 2, 1-6; 3, 17-24; 10, 8-18). Slavery was such a natural thing that the Psalmist could pray, 'As the eyes of a slave are on the hands of his master, so our eyes are fixed on the Lord our God until he has mercy on us' (Ps 123, 2).

This social myth of slavery was still very much in force at the time of Christ. He himself does not contradict it in any single text. In fact, he introduced slaves into his parables for the sake of comparison. We are told to be like slaves that are faithful to their master even when he is not at home and who stay up to welcome him on his return (Lk 12, 42-48). Jesus seems to condone the custom of slavery when he says, 'Which of you, with a slave ploughing or minding sheep, would say to him when he returns from the field, "Come and have your meal immediately"? Would he not be more likely to say, "Get my supper laid; make yourself tidy and wait on me while I eat and drink. You can eat and drink yourself afterwards"? Must he be grateful to the slave for doing what he was told? So with you: when you have done all you have been told to do, say "We are merely slaves; we have done no more than our duty" ' (Lk 17, 7-10). Christ simply accepted slavery as a reality.

The same must be said about the early Church. The apostles instructed their christian slaves to be obedient to their masters, not to rebel against them. 'Slaves must be respectful and obedient to their masters, not only when they are kind and gentle but also when they are unfair' (1 Pet 2, 18-20). 'Slaves, be obedient to the men who are called your masters in this world; not only when you are under their eye, as if you had only to please men, but wholeheartedly, out of respect for the Master' (Col 3, 22-25). 'Slaves, be obedient to the men who are called your masters in this world, with deep respect and sincere loyalty, as you are obedient to Christ' (Eph 6, 5-8; see also 1 Tim 6, 1-2; Tit 2, 9-10). Also the terminology of slavery is often used in religious symbolism. Redemption is understood as a liberation from the slavery of sin (Rom 6, 6; Jn 8, 34; etc.). Christians are called the 'slaves of Christ' (Gal 4, 5; 3, 13; Rom 1, 1; etc.). Even the Incarnation is formulated as the Son assuming the form of a slave (Phil 2, 7).

Now it would be easy to argue from all this scriptural material that the institution of slavery is part of revealed doctrine. God himself wanted slavery: 'In the fulness of his wisdom the Lord has made distinctions between man and man and diversified their conditions' (Sir 33, 11). Christ could have spoken out against slavery but did not do so. This must have been deliberate and so, accepting slavery, he established it as a norm according to which society should be judged. The apostles recognised the distinction of masters and slaves among their own christians as a valid one with corresponding duties devolving on each according to his status. Such were the arguments of traditional theology that remained unchallenged until abolitionists forced the Church to re-examine its doctrine on the matter.

Recognising social myth: the dawn of light

It is amazing how long the official view of the Church concerning slavery was maintained and also how quickly the new insight took over once it had gained ground. As late as 1866 the Holy Office issued an Instruction that justified slavery. After mentioning that the Holy See had often forbidden the negro slave trade as unjust kidnapping, the document proceeds:

> 'Nevertheless, slavery itself, considered as such in its essential nature, is not at all contrary to the natural and divine law, and there can be several just titles of slavery and these are referred to by approved theologians and commentators of the sacred canons. . . . It is not contrary to the natural and divine law for a slave to be sold, bought, exchanged or given. . . .'.[53]

The Holy Office thus declared ordinary slavery to be sanctioned by Scripture (divine law). Twenty-five years later, in 1891, Pope Leo XIII issued the encyclical *Rerum Novarum* in which any legitimate excuse for slavery was denied. In 1918 the new Code of Canon Law imposed heavy ecclesiastical penalties on whoever 'sells a human being into slavery' (can. 2354). In 1965 Vatican stated:

> 'All offences against human dignity: such as... arbitrary imprisonment, deportation, slavery... the traffic in women and children... all these and the like are criminal. They poison civilisation; and they debase the perpetrators more than the victims and militates against the honour of the creator.'[54]

Behind these dates lies a dramatic evolution of thoUght. Contemporary social liberation acted as a welcome stimulus. From accepting (domestic) slavery as a normal feature of life people changed to seeing it for what it is: an unjustice against human persons. But it also involved the recognition that Scripture had been read the wrong way. That, although Christ accepted slavery as a reality, he did not thereby condone it as a legitimate practice.

The basic equality of all human persons was implicit in the fact that Christ's redemption was meant for every creature (Mk 16, 15). For Christ redemption meant liberation from any form of slavery. All differences of status between men are broken down. Strictly speaking, a christian should not be a slave. All this, we now recognise, is closer to the heart of Christ's message than the acceptance of slavery. The lesson is that we should be extremely careful when scriptural authors speak from a social myth of their own times. The myth itself is not part of the doctrine.

Theologians come to their senses

To come back to the immediate topic in hand, we observe that a similar process is at work. There are quite a few scholars who continue to consider the traditional arguments from Scripture against the ordination of women as valid as ever. To mention a number by name: Ph. Delhaye (1972), F. P. Chenderlin (1972) and J. Galot (1973).[55] We may also safely reckon that those inclined to hold on to the old arguments may not feel the need to publish their views as much as do those who disagree.

On the other hand, no one familiar with the theological scene can deny that among scholars a landslide is taking place in favour of a new scriptural understanding. Theologians doing independent researches all over the world come to the same conclusion: Christ adapted to the custom of his time; he did not lay down a norm regarding women priests. To ascribe this to 'an itch for novelty' or 'a desire to accommodate', is to do an injustice to many conscientious men. As in so many other instances of the past, we are witnessing a moment when theology comes to its senses.

Why did Christ not choose a woman for the college of apostles? G. R. Evans, Bishop of Denver and member of the USA Bishops' Subcommittee on Women in Church and Society, writes (1972):

> 'The sociocultural pattern of his time has to be kept in mind. Why did Christ not choose a slave for the apostolic college? Such a choice would have halted the practice of the Church refusing to ordain slaves for a long time. Why did not Christ choose a gentile for the college? Such an action could have more easily avoided much bitter debate in the early Church. A matter of fact need not be a matter of right. One cannot draw conclusions as to the rights involved from the mere observation of the state of affairs.'[56]

The non-fact of Christ not having selected women should not be seen as expressing Christ's mind and will.

> 'If Jesus had lived in a society in which the cultural status of the two sexes had differed from that of his own time, would he not have made a different choice? A choice that was already beginning to show itself in the completely new approach which he adopted toward women in a patriarchal society?' (H. M. Legrand 1977).[57]

51

'To have gone further and called six men and six women to make up the twelve would have outraged his contemporaries to the point of destroying his work from the outset.' (G. O'Collins 1974). [58]

'There is just this fact: Jesus chose only men to be his apostles. We are left to discern why. And I would contend that it is gratuitous to assert that this was because it is the will of God that for all time only males be chosen for the role of apostle or bishop or priest, i.e. for the ministry of leadership in preaching the gospel and celebrating the liturgy and governing the community. Rather I would argue that it is much more cogent to surmise that Jesus chose only men to be his apostles simply because only men could then function in such a role of leadership due to the cultural conditions of the age. However, it is quite obvious that such cultural conditions can pass; and so with them can pass also the rationale for limiting this ministry of leadership to men only.' (E. C. Meyer 1976).[59]

The number of theological studies confirming this trend of thought increases year by year. To restrict myself to a few examples from the seventies, in chronological order: J. L. Acebal, J. J. Begley-Armbruster, R. Gryson, I. Raming, J. M. Ford, R. Metz, F. Klostermann, J. M. Aubert.[60] Y. Congar hesitates. In 1970 he wrote: 'It is not certain that the exclusion of women is of divine law'.[61] In 1971: 'I would simply say that, to my view, the prohibition of the feminine priesthood is not of divine law. But I add: what authorises one to say that this restriction is only of a socio-cultural nature? I deny that one can say this with absolute certainty.'[62] Cardinal J. Danielou on the other hand was quite outspoken on seeing no theological obstacle to the ordination of women.[63] K. Rahner, who had guided H. van der Meer in his thorough doctoral study on the subject (published in 1962), stated recently:

'The practice which the Catholic Church has of not ordaining women to the priesthood has no binding theological character.... The actual practice is not a dogma. It is purely and simply based on a human and historic reflection which was valid in the past in cultural and social conditions which are presently changing rapidly.'[64]

At this juncture some of my readers may suspect that I am bolstering up my own arguments with an appeal to other scholars. Although such confirmation is of course always welcome, it is not the reason for the incomplete survey of literature given above. The theme of this chapter concerns scriptural argumentation itself. The question asked was: why do scholars disagree among themselves? The implication is that, as long as theologians take different sides, the scriptural evidence remains undecided. It is this question I should now like to tackle.

It is only natural that there will be discussion among theologians for a long time to come. Old ideas are not easily abandoned. It takes much thought and research before a new scriptural insight is universally accepted. Theology is slow by nature. If I may refer once more to the theology of slavery, we find that some Catholic theologians continued to defend slavery until the middle of the XXth century.[65] What A. Cochin remarked in the course of his plea for changing one's view on slavery (in 1861) still holds good:

'Predisposed to show respect for tradition, theologians are especially anxious to attach themselves to the chain of the past, and to rest their doctrines on those which were professed before them; a valuable, or rather, indispensable, tendency when points of faith are in question — a dangerous tendency when it regards open questions, the solution of which changes and is susceptible of progress. They teach concerning slavery what was taught yesterday and the day before, but what no priest or layman believes any longer today ...'[66]

In other words: we need not be surprised if some theologians still continue to reject the insights of new research. What should decide the matter is the value of the scriptural arguments themselves. The fact of disagreemnt on interpretation, of search and debate, does not by itself invalidate the scriptural evidence. We need the courage to look afresh at Scripture and to ask new questions.

6 WOULD PAUL NOT RAISE HIS EYEBROWS?

'. . . Disciplinary practices of minor importance, such as the obligation imposed upon women to wear a veil on the head (1 Cor 11, 2-16) . . . no longer have a normative value. However, the Apostle's forbidding women "to speak" in the assemblies (cf 1 Cor 14, 34-35; 1 Tim 2, 12) is of a different nature, and exegetes define its meaning in this way: Paul in no way opposes the right, which he elsewhere recognises as possessed by women, to prophesy in the assembly (cf 1 Cor 11, 5); the prohibition solely concerns the official function of teaching in the christian assembly.

For Saint Paul this prescription is bound up with the divine plan of creation (cf 1 Cor 11, 7; Gen 2, 18-24); it would be difficult to see in it the expression of a cultural fact. Nor should it be forgotten that we owe to Saint Paul one of the most vigorous texts in the New Testament on the fundamental equality of men and women, as children of God in christ (cf Gal 3, 28). Therefore there is no reason for accusing him of prejudice against women. . . .'.

(Roman Document on Women Priests.)

In my opinion we have here a classical example of how theology can misjudge the value of a biblical text. Paul did indeed forbid women to speak or to teach with authority during the weekly assembly. He did this in conformity with Jewish custom. He supported his point with a theological rationalisation. Neither Paul's prohibition nor his rationalisation is binding on us today. The prohibition concerned a passing custom that could be adjusted in changed conditions.

The rationalisation served the need of the moment and did not contribute points of doctrine.

We speak of 'rationalising' when we try to justify an emotional attitude with a rational argument. Many Whites have an instinctive distrust of Blacks. They will justify this prejudice with a series of logical arguments, adducing cases where Negroes have proved untrustworthy, etc., whereas in fact their distrust is based on an emotional reason. Activists who are always ready to take on more work from an inner necessity to keep themselves occupied, will try to prove to others as well as to themselves that the work is forced on them from outside. A woman who for some instinctive reasons does not like a particular man will, on demand, produce rationalisations for her dislike. Rationalising means: convincing ourselves of having intellectual reasons for a view we have emotionally adopted.

Rationalisation also occurs in Scripture. It should be recognised as such; otherwise we may mistake it for teaching. The social custom of treating the seventh day as holy and a day of rest existed more than a thousand years before the rationalising explanation, 'For in six days Yahweh made the heavens and the earth and the sea and all that these hold but on the seventh day he rested; that is why Yahweh has blessed the sabbath day and made it sacred' (Ex 20, 11; see also Gen 2, 1-3). The literal meaning of the words would suggest that the six-days' creation is an historical fact and the observance of the sabbath is an obligation deriving from it. However, it is really the other way about. Finding the observance of the sabbath of so great importance, the author deduces, 'meditates', that it must be so because of the way in which God has created the world.

God thirsting for blood?

Or consider the following incident from David's life. A severe famine of three years ravaged the country. A popular oracle attributed this famine to unrequited blood vengeance.

56

Saul had committed some atrocity against Gibeon for which the Gibeonites had not been allowed to take revenge. 'The Lord said: "There is blood guilt on Saul and his house" (2 Sam 21, 1). To make up for this, David ordered that seven innocent descendants of Saul should be killed and hung on gibbets. Through this the famine was halted. 'After that God heeded supplications from the land' (2 Sam 21, 14).

If one reads the story superficially, one has the impression that Scripture attributes to God some remarkably vindictive action. God is dissatisfied because the Gibeonites did not get a chance to take blood vengeance on the family of Saul. So God inflicts a famine on the whole country. He does not lift the punishment until seven descendants of Saul's house have been executed. A lot of questions come to mind: if God is so angry about it, why did he take action only so many years after the crime? Why should he punish the whole country if only one man, now dead, had been guilty? Is blood vengeance of such great moral value that its practice needs safeguarding at all costs? Why should God take pleasure in the execution of seven innocent descendants of Saul if, elsewhere, it is stated in the Law: 'Fathers may not be put to death for their sons, nor sons for their fathers. Each is to be put to death for his own sin' (Dt 24,16)?

The whole text is obviously a rationalisation. Whenever a famine occurred, people would ascribe it to God's anger. Searching for a cause, they might stumble on the Gibeonites' claim to blood vengeance and imagine this to be the reason why God is angry. When rains fell after the execution of the seven innocent men, it was again understood as a sign of reconciliation on the part of God. Such rationalisations are quite understandable and human, but we should beware of seeing in them *teaching* on God or on his will.

Wearing a veil

Paul wanted women to wear a veil when christians met together in common assembly. It was a Jewish custom to which some women at Corinth had taken exception. Paul devotes a lengthy argument to it, producing the one theological rationalisation after the other: man does not need to wear a veil because he is more directly related to Christ; man is the image of God and reflects God's glory; man was the first to be created; woman depends on man in all these things. Paul himself realises the weakness of all this theologising and finally comes to the point when he states: 'To anyone who might still want to argue: it is not the custom with us, nor in the assemblies of God' (1 Cor 11, 1-6).

Paul is one of the greatest theologians of the New Testament. But he certainly slipped up on this passage. In his anxiety to justify the common practice of women wearing a veil, he allows himself to be dragged into theological speculations that are typically Jewish, not Christian. Some of his arguments we cannot even fully understand as they presuppose Jewish theology no longer available to us. Why would a man 'disrespect his head' if he prays with his head covered, and a woman 'disrespect her head' if she prays unveiled? Why should a woman cover her head 'out of respect for the angels'? St Paul is on thin ice here and it would be unfair to him and incorrect in theology to take his argument seriously. The most we can say is that, in his rationalisation, Paul shows how much he is still imbued with the jewish social myth of male predominance.

Speaking in the Assembly

Another Pauline custom that belongs to this category concerns women speaking in the public assembly. Although Paul finds it normal for a woman to pray or prophesy in the assembly (1 Cor 11, 5), he forbids her 'to speak':

> 'As in all the churches of the saints, women are to remain quiet at meetings since they have no permission to speak; they must keep in the background as the Law itself lays down. If they have any questions to ask, they

should ask their husbands at home: it does not seem right for a woman to raise her voice at a meeting' (1 Cor 14, 34-35).

'During instruction, a woman should be quiet and respectful. I am not giving permission for a woman to teach or to tell a man what to do. A woman ought not to speak, because Adam was formed first and Eve afterwards, and it was not Adam who was led astray but the woman was led astray and fell into sin' (1 Tim 2, 12-14).

These texts were made much of in scholastic theology to prove that women could not be given any authority in the Church. Cornelius a Lapide, writing in 1616, expressed common opinion when he called the prohibition for women to speak: 'absolute and universal'. He listed five reasons for this prohibition:

1. It follows from woman's nature and God's positive command in Genesis 3, 16.
2. Silence is more suitable to woman's humble status in the presence of men.
3. Man possesses better reason and judgment and more discretion than woman.
4. By speaking, woman may be tempted to lead man to sin.
5. It is better that women should remain ignorant of what is not necessary. By asking stupid questions in church she would give scandal to others.[67]

Cornelius' exegesis was obviously tainted with prejudice. He read more into the text than is warranted because he was anxious to see it confirm what he already believed. But, if we condemn this, does the Roman document in its argumentation not merit a similar judgment? Does the document not overstate the importance of the passage because it is anxious to find a text excluding women from ordination? Why would wearing a veil be of less importance than speaking in the assembly? Paul devotes many more verses to the former than to the latter custom. Why would Paul's wish that women attend the meeting with heads covered be time-bound whereas his refusal to let women speak would amount to an exclusion of women from priestly service on doctrinal grounds? Can this momentous differentiation really be proved from Scripture itself?

The official commentary on the Roman document has a phrase that makes one suspect it was the traditional use of the text in mediaeval theology that determined its sense. The similarity with Cornelius' exegesis may be more than accidental! 'Theologians have made abundant use of these texts (1 Cor 14, 34-35; 1 Tim 2, 11-14) to explain that women cannot receive either the power of magisterium or that of jurisdiction. It was especially the text of 1 Timothy that provided St Thomas with the proof that woman is in a state of submission or service, since (as the text explains) woman was created after man and was the person first responsible for original sin.'[68] In other words: because theologians like Thomas Aquinas and Cornelius a Lapide understood the text in this way, we too should understand it as such. But, as I have shown before, and as the document admits, the theologians of the Middle Ages were biased against women and often drew wrong conclusions from these same texts. Thomas Aquinas had such strange ideas about the sexes that, commenting on 1 Cor 11, he could say that nuns who take vows 'are promoted to the dignity of men.'[69] Is he then, in the present context, a safe guide to judge Scripture passages by? Or to turn the argument: if Thomas had known the modern exegesis on the subject state of women in 1 Tim 2, 11-14, would he himself not revise his stand on women's ordination? His reason for stating that women cannot be ordained is that 'It is not possible for the female sex to signify eminence of degree as it is characterised by the state of submission.'[70] In judging these difficult Scripture texts the scholastics are better left alone, because they too lived in a male dominated social system.

Bound up with creation?

The document on this same subject of women speaking in the assembly also states: 'For Saint Paul the prescription is bound up with the divine plan of creation (cf 1 Cor 11, 7; Gen 2, 18-24); it would be difficult to see in it the expression of a cultural fact.' Can this enormous doctrinal weight so ascribed to the verse be deduced from the theological reason attached to the prohibition? And what about the fact that Paul attaches the same reason to the wearing of the veil? The same consideration, namely that Adam was created before Eve is adduced by Paul to prove that women should wear a veil (1 Cor 11, 8-10) and that she should not speak in the assembly (1 Tim 2, 12-13). Should not the same judgment be applied to both?

There is no reason to doubt the historical fact that Paul did not allow women to teach in the church assemblies. Many of these early christians were either Jews or proselytes, so allowing women to teach was neither opportune nor, perhaps, possible. As in the question of wearing a veil, so here too Paul adds a theological rationalisation to the custom. And again it is a typically Jewish one. He refers to Mosaic Law: 'As the law itself says.' He refers to the creation account according to which Adam was created before Eve. However such a rationalisation has no teaching value and cannot carry the weight of a full doctrinal statement. The Law of Moses had been abolished with Christ as St. Paul himself frequently affirms. Who came first and who last at creation was a favourite topic of discussion among Jewish theologians, which led Paul in other texts to compare Christ to Adam (see 1 Cor 15, 45-49). When the Roman document says that for Paul the prohibition was 'bound up with the divine plan of creation,' it over values the weight of the text. Instead of proclaiming the enormous doctrine ascribed to it ('woman cannot exercise authority in the Church because that is the way God created her'), it contains the rationalisation of a great apostle who could, at times, not refrain from indulging in the theological pastimes he had been used to as a rabbi.

7 THE IMPLICATIONS OF CHRIST'S PRIESTHOOD

It is all very well to defend women and all that, but would a woman priest be really compatible with Christ's priesthood? After all, Christ was a man. When the priest says Mass, he is, so to say, the image of Christ within the community. Could you imagine a woman standing at the altar who would remind you of Christ in the way a man can do so?

Certainly, some women may like to think of themselves as priests. Ordaining women might give a great uplift to them and might make the Church more popular in contemporary society. But are we allowed to sacrifice the sign value of the priesthood to such human considerations? I feel that the Church should not compromise Christ's priesthood, even if it may hurt some people.

The above sentiments are also expressed in the Roman document though phrased in less colloquial terms. They force us to consider Christ's priesthood itself. Would it suffer from representation by a woman? Is a man, because he is a man, by nature more suited to exercise a priestly function 'in the person of Christ'? Is the male character an intrinsic element in Christ's priesthood? In the words of the Roman document: '. . . . In human beings the difference of sex exercises an important influence, much deeper than, for example, ethnic differences; the latter do not affect the human person as intimately as the difference of sex — We can never ignore the fact that Christ is a man. And therefore, unless one is to disregard the importance of this symbolism for the economy of Revelation . . . his role (this is the original meaning of the word *persona*) must be taken by a man.'

It is my considered view that Scripture does not allow us to infer that the difference of sex plays a part in Christ's priesthood. Christ replaced a priesthood based on sacrality by a priesthood based on grace. It would be illogical to imply that discriminations wiped out by baptism should be revived in the sacramental priesthood. If every christian radiates Christ through his life, there seems to be no reason why every christian could not be commissioned to represent him at the Eucharist. The sacramental sign of the priesthood is the human personality of the ordained priest, whether man or woman. Sacred Scripture itself does not explicitly teach that women can be ordained. But it does seem a logical inference from the nature of Christ's priesthood, that women could and should partake in the sacramental priesthood.

A priesthood without 'sacred' realities

Jesus was not a social reformer. He did not want to take part in the social revolution. The same cannot be said about his involvement in religion. Though he was tolerant and accommodating regarding the social structures of his time, he was intolerant regarding antiquated and inadequate religious structures. In this field his action could hardly have been more ruthless. He utterly abolished the priesthood as understood in Old Testament terms.

To understand the full implications of Jesus' attitude in this matter, we should recall that the Old Testament priesthood rested on a philosophy that distinguished between the sacred and the profane. Some everyday realities, such as houses, cattle, eating and sleeping, doing business, and so on, were ordinary or 'profane.' God was not really directly present in these realities. Other realities of our world however were considered to have been penetrated with God's presence and to have become 'sacred' on that account. This is the origin of 'sacred' times (the sabbath and feastdays), 'sacred' places (mainly the Temple), 'sacred' objects (e.g. vessels used for worship) and 'sacred' persons (priests) consecrated to God.

The Old Testament priest was separated from other men on the same basis as the sabbath was considered holier than the Monday, or the Temple was a more sacred place than the Pool of Bethzatha. The priest was the embodiment of a divine presence in a profane world.

Instead of substituting new holy realities for the old ones, Christ went further. He radically abrogated the distinction itself between the sacred and the profane. This may seem startling to some christians who unconsciously continue to think along Old Testament lines. They may imagine the New Testament to be an updated version of the Old. They think our churches have taken the place of the Temple at Jerusalem, that our Sunday replaces the sabbath, that our sacred vessels continue the Temple furniture and that the New Testament priest is a polished version of the Old Testament one. The cause of this misunderstanding is partly due to developments within the Church in the course of her history, partly in deference towards the human necessity of having quasi-sacred realities like churches as part of an established religion. But basically the clinging to 'sacred' realities is a regression and contrary to the teaching of the New Testament.

Take the example of *sacred place*. The Jews were allowed to sacrifice only in the Temple (Dt 12, 1-14) and, even within the Temple, place became holier the nearer one approached its centre. The inner chamber of the sanctuary, called 'Holy of Holies,' could be entered only by the high priest and then only once a year (Heb 9, 71). Christ no longer acknowledges such holy places. He sanctified all place. In his kingdom, worship can be given not only in Jerusalem or on a holy mountain, but anywhere so long as it is done 'in spirit and in truth' (Jn 4, 20-24). In fact, his own body was the new temple that could substitute for the old in any part of the world (Jn 2, 21). When Christ celebrated Mass for the first time at the Last Supper, he did so in the upper room of an ordinary house (Mk 14, 12-16). To crown it all, the place he chose for bringing his unique sacrifice for the whole world was not the

Temple court but an ugly hill of execution (Heb 14, 12). When Christ died, the distinction between sacred and profane places was wiped out once and for all. The Gospels record that the curtain of the Temple, which screened off the 'Holy of Holies,' 'was torn in two, from top to bottom' (Mk 15,37). The early Church realised this. They had no temples, churches or chapels. They celebrated common prayer and the Eucharist wherever they gathered as a community. The same has basically remained true of the Church today, even though the custom of setting aside places for prayer has crept in again from the fourth century.

The same holds good for *sacred days*. For the Jews, the sabbath was a day consecrated to God on which man was not allowed to work for his own profit. Jesus frequently clashed with the Pharisees because he refused to suspend his apostolate on the sabbath. Conflicts arose when his disciples plucked ears of corn (Mt 12. 1-8), when Jesus cured a man with a withered hand in the synagogue (Mk 13, 6), when he healed a man who had dropsy (Lk 14, 1-6), and when he gave sight to the blind man at Siloam (Jn 9, 1-16). Jesus' most revolutionary statement in the discussion was: 'The sabbath was made for man, not man for the sabbath' (Mk 2, 27). In other words, the sabbath does not derive its value from itself, from being 'sacred' time of some kind or other, but from serving a human need.

Whereas the Old Testament priests had to offer frequently at specified sacral times, Christ sanctified the totality of time by his all-sufficient sacrifice (Heb 9, 25-28). With Jesus' death the sabbath and all these sacral times had become meaningless (Gal 4, 8-11). From now on, any day and any hour of the day could be the appropriate time for prayer and celebration. The christian practice of celebrating the Eucharist on 'the first day of the week' because Christ rose on that day (Jn 20, 1) led to the practice of weekly Mass on Sundays. However, the Sunday was not a new 'sabbath' for them. It is again by an unfortunate return to the Old Testament that christians of later centuries, and particularly in Protestant churches, reverted to a Sunday observance patterned on a pharisaic model.

Having seen Christ's attitude towards sacred time and place, we will not be surprised to see his same attitude towards sacred priesthood. He abolished the priesthood as a sacral institution. He himself did not belong to the priesthood of Aaron. As representative of all men, he abolished that priestly dignity which was linked to bodily descent. He established a new priesthood built on 'the power of indestructible life' (Heb 7, 16). The Old Testament notions of the priesthood were so alien to Christ that we never find him applying the term priest to himself or his followers. In fact, it is only in the letter to the Hebrews that the 'priesthood' of Christ is discussed in explicit terms and compared with the priesthood of the Old Testament (see especially Heb 5, 1-4; 7, 26-28). Christ entrusted a special task to his apostles and their successors, but he would not have agreed to this ministry being understood as setting apart a new sacred group as had been the case in Old Testament times. The later developments in the Church which favoured such a separation (with 'sacred' vestments, clerical dignities and status prerogatives) would certainly have alarmed and saddened him.

A priesthood in which all share

Christ exercised his priesthood by offering himself on Calvary and by preaching. To continue these two ministeries, every disciple has to carry His cross (Mt 6, 24); each of his followers has to bear witness to him even unto persecution and death (Mt 10, 16-22). All christians therefore participate in the royal priesthood of Christ (1 Pet 2, 5-9). All can be called 'priests to his God and Father' (Rev 1, 6), 'priests of God and of Christ' (Rev 20, 6). All together they constitute 'a kingdom and priesthood to our God' (Rev 5, 10).

This common priesthood is given through the sacrament of baptism. We should note that this baptism is exactly the same for every single person. There is absolutely no difference in the baptism conferred on women. St Paul affirms that the baptism of Christ transcends and obliterates whatever social differences exist among mankind. 'It is through faith that all of you are God's children in union with Christ Jesus. For all who are baptised into the union of Christ have taken upon themselves the qualities of Christ himself. So there is no difference between Jews and Gentiles, between slaves and free men, between men and women . . . You are all one in union with Christ Jesus' (Gal 3, 26-28).

The ordination to the sacramental priesthood is an extension of the basic sacrificial and prophetic sharing that has already been given in baptism. Although the ministerial priesthood adds a new function to the powers received in baptism, and is thus substantially more than baptism, it is at the same time intrinsically related to it.

> 'Though they differ essentially and not only in degree, the common priesthood of the faithful and the ministerial or hierarchical priesthood are none the less ordered one to the other; each in its own way shares in the one priesthood of Christ.'[71]

When the Council says that the sharing in Christ's priesthood through the sacrament of Holy Orders is *essentially* different, it means that baptism by itself does not confer the commission to teach, rule and offer sacrfice in the name of Christ. It does not mean to say that for Holy Orders a different set of discriminating values would hold good.

Whatever may be required for ordination to the ministry, it cannot be a 'sacred' reality that would make one person intrinsically superior to another. Vatican II is explicit on this:

> 'There is a common dignity of members deriving from their rebirth in Christ, a common grace as children, a common vocation to perfection, one salvation, one hope and undivided charity. In Christ and in the Church there is, then, no inequality arising from race or nationality, social condition or sex. . . .

Although by Christ's will some are established as teachers, dispensers of the mysteries and pastors for the others, there remains, nevertheless, a true equality between all with regard to the dignity and the activity that is common to all the faithful in the building up of the Body of Christ.'[72]

But if sex cannot be a limiting factor as a 'sacred' reality or as a remnant of pre-baptismal inequality, how can it play a role on the level of the sacramental sign?

A priesthood of love

The claim that Christ is represented better by a man because Christ too was a man cannot be substantiated from any scriptural text. The argument given in the Roman document is of a philosophical nature. It is what is known in theology as an argument based on convenience or, as the document puts it, 'showing the profound fittingness that theological reflection discovers.' The substance of the argument is found in these words:

' "Sacramental signs," says St Thomas, "represent what they signify by natural resemblance." The same natural resemblance is required for persons as for things; when Christ's role in the Eucharist is to be expressed sacramentally, there would not be this natural resemblance which must exist between Christ and his minister if the role of Christ were not taken by a man: in such a case it would be difficult to see in the minister the image of Christ. For Christ himself was and remains a man.'

The argument is wrong because the philosophy it pre-supposes is wrong. The scholastics, to whom the document refers as the source of the argument, propounded a philosophy of the sexes that can no longer be defended by any christian. St Bonaventure (also quoted in the document) maintained that only the male person presents a true image of

God.[73] Because woman is only an 'incomplete man'[74] and thus 'cannot signify eminence of degree,'[75] St Thomas concluded that she could not 'resemble' Christ or be his 'image'. But surely such reasoning contradicts Scripture itself, let alone a better philosophy of human dignity. God's Word links both sexes when speaking of divine resemblance: 'God created man in the image of himself; in the image of God he created him; male and female he created them' (Gen 2,27). And St Paul says that all, men and women, have put on Christ (Gal 2, 27). He speaks of all christians when he says, 'We, with our unveiled faces reflecting like mirrors the brightness of the Lord, all grow brighter and brighter as we are turned into the image that we reflect; this is the work of the Lord who is Spirit' (2 Cor 3, 18).

As to the symbolism of God in the Old Testament and of Christ in the New, as Bridegroom etc., such symbolism belongs basically to the Jewish context. It cannot be shown to be essential to the priesthood of Christ. What is more, Scripture itself transcends male symbolism in more than one case. The Bible stresses that there are feminine aspects to God's compassion. God's everlasting fidelity is compared to the never-forgetting love of a mother for her children (Is 49, 15). Christ is spoken of as being tender (Heb 5, 2) and anxious as a hen wanting to protect her chickens (Mt 23, 37). Even Paul speaks of himself as a mother (1 Thes 2, 7; Gal 4, 19).

By stressing the male sex as such an essential characteristic of the priesthood, are we not undervaluing the priesthood of Christ? What are the features described by Scripture itself as pre-eminent in signifying Christ's presence? If we go by the qualifications seen in Jesus, the high priest, we find the following to be of paramount importance in his priesthood:

1. to be called by God (Heb 5, 4);
2. having suffered himself, to be able to help those who are tempted (Heb 5, 1-2);

3. to be able to sympathise with people's weaknesses (Heb 4, 14-16);
4. to be able to deal gently with the ignorant and the wayward (Heb 5, 1-10).

This is quite different from requiring that he be a (male!) descendant of Aaron. It is indeed a new priesthood ruled by its own law (Heb 7, 11-12).[76]

Listening to Christ himself we hear him stress love as the sign he requires. By laying down his life for his friends Christ proved his love (Jn 15, 12-13). It is by such love that the true shepherd is distinguished from the hireling (Jn 10, 11-15). Readiness to serve, not the power to dominate, makes one to be like Christ (Mt 20, 24-28). Not by presiding at table alone but by washing people's feet is the Master recognised (Jn 13, 12-16). One should note that we are not dealing here with a mere moral requirement but with an element that has sign value. 'By this love you have for one another, everyone will know that you are my disciples' (Jn 13, 35). Although Christ is speaking of love as a commandment, he is here addressing the apostles on the very occasion he is ordaining them as his priests. His 'Do this in memory of Me' presupposes pastoral love as the special sign by which his disciples should be recognised. It is such love he demands from Peter before entrusting him with the apostolic commission (Jn 21, 15-17).

Such considerations do not directly prove that women could be ordained priests. They demonstrate, however, that Scripture itself lays stress on values such as sympathy, service and love rather than on accidentals like being a man, even on the level of the sacramental sign. Would we not be nearer to Christ's mind when we stipulate that a woman filled with the spirit of Christ's pastoral love is a more 'fitting' image of his presence than a man who were to lack such love?

8   A VISION OF THINGS
TO COME IN LUKE'S GOSPEL

You have stressed that Jesus conformed to the Jewish notion of woman's role in society. I can see the importance of recognising this fact as it proves that he did not deliberately exclude women from the ministry. Yet it leaves me dissatisfied. Did Jesus overlook the injustice done to women in his times? Had he no sympathy with woman and her specific task in life? Was Jesus so absorbed in addressing men that he failed to give a special message to women?

I realise that it would be wrong to read our contemporary problematics into the Gospel text. Yet I would feel encouraged if I knew that my search for a true evaluation of woman's place in society and the Church was rooted in the Gospel. It would be a matter of great support to me if I knew that Jesus was concerned about women and that his words and actions can be seen to justify woman's emancipation. Does nothing that Jesus said or did point, however remotely, to the possibility of future ministry by women? What has the Gospel to say about this?

The Gospel has a lot to say that can rightly give courage to women. Luke's Gospel in particular is certainly concerned about their special role. Although Christ refused to be a social reformer in this as in other fields, many of his words and actions show that woman's participation in the ministry would not be contrary to his mind.

So far I have based my argumentation from Scripture on a narrow interpretation of the text. This is unavoidable as we are dealing with a *theological* argument that should be able to withstand the scrutiny of critics. Arguments are based on proofs, proofs on undeniable evidence. In argumentation one is limited to mutually accepted premises, to a logic that will convince one's adversary, to an analytical and restrictive form of thinking. In this chapter, however, I should like to proceed beyond this and approach the gospel in a more reflective mood. I should like to penetrate into its core; listen attentively to what it says by implication as well as by express statement; capture intuitively the deeper insights of the inspired message.

Mary of Magdala

Let us turn to St Luke's Gospel and study the history of Mary of Magdala. She had led a sinful life but had been converted by Jesus. 'Mary, known as Mary of Magdala, from whom seven devils had come out' (Lk 8, 2). Luke narrates about her that she was among the women who accompanied Jesus on his apostolic tours (Lk 8, 1-3); that with other disciples she watched the crucifixion of Jesus and helped at his burial (Lk 23, 49. 55-56); that she was among the first to learn about the resurrection on Easter morning (Lk 24, 1-11). In the Acts of the Apostles Luke makes Peter express the following requirement for a person to fit into the apostolic team: 'One of us who bore us company all the while we had the Lord Jesus with us, coming and going, from John's ministry of baptism until the day he was taken up from us — one of those must join us now as a witness to his resurrection' (Acts 1, 21-22). If we go by this requirement Mary of Magdala *could* have qualified, as well as many other persons who did not belong to the original Twelve. Mary witnessed Jesus' public ministry, his passion and resurrection. It may be objected that she was not present at the Last Supper. But neither was Matthias who was eventually chosen to take Judas's place.

Mary of Magdala could not have taken up the position of an Apostle for the social reasons I have explained before. But not because she did not fulfil the requirements of the Gospel. I believe that especially in St Luke's gospel we have here a

74

vision of possibilities that goes much beyond the social limitations of the time. Recall the episode of the sinful woman who weeps at Jesus' feet as he reclines in a Pharisee's house (Lk 7, 36-50). She may historically have been Mary of Magdala; in Luke's eyes she certainly is the same kind of person (see the connection with 8, 1-3). About her Jesus says:

> 'You see this woman?
> I came to your house:
> you provided no water for my feet;
> but this woman has made my feet wet with her tears
> and wiped then with her hair.
> You gave me no kiss;
> but she has been kissing my feet ever since I came in.
> You did not anoint my head with oil;
> but she has anointed my feet with myrhh.'

It is as if Jesus is speaking to us across the centuries. 'What is all this discussion,' he might say, 'about women in the ministry? What makes you think I would turn her away from the sanctuary or from my altar? Have I not always stressed the real thing rather than accidentals? When I was in the house of Simon the Pharisee, did I not praise the sinful woman for exercising the ministry of the footwashing? It was not her status, nor her previous sins, but her love that counted in my eyes. By her kiss of welcome, by washing my feet, by her gift of ointment, it was she who was my minister at that moment more than all the men who sat around. Would I refuse any woman to be my minister who could serve my Body, the Church, in the same way: by breaking the bread, by pouring the water of baptism or anointing the sick? Don't you think I am happy that women in your time are at last given that position in society that is rightly theirs? Would I not recognise the real contribution a woman priest can make in the new world you are living in now?'

At this point I may have lost credibility. Is it correct to read Scripture in this way? Do the passages on Mary of Magdala *intend* to give a vision of new ministries or is such an interpretation nothing more than wishful thinking? To reply adequately I will have to say a little more about Luke's theology. I should like to demonstrate the following points:

Luke is concerned about the exaggerated expectations of his contemporaries regarding the Last Day. He teaches that before Christ's coming we should recognise *the period of the Church*.

Luke points out that we can expect *new developments* during this period of the Church. These new developments, though not explicitly contained in Jesus' message, have yet a divine origin. They derive from the action of the Holy Spirit within the Church.

Luke is convinced that many of these new developments are *implicitly contained* in what Jesus said or did. When writing his Gospel, Luke sees in many events of Jesus' life a vision of things to come.

Luke wants to stress that it was natural for the Early Church to develop *new ministries*. The focus on women in Luke's Gospel points to possibilities of their future participation in the ministry.

This seems a rather long path to travel. It is well worth the trouble. *If* Luke teaches, as I will show to be the case, that we should expect new developments in the Church, also regarding the ministry; and *if* Luke himself in this context points to the role of women, may we choose to disregard this message? It would seem that, under inspiration, Luke is precisely speaking about the question that is now before us: can there be in the Church a new participation of women in the ministry, not explicitly foreseen in the Gospel? Luke's answer would be a categorical 'Yes'.

No room for the Church?

After the resurrection of Jesus it took the apostolic community quite some time to realise that a new era had begun, the era of the Church.

Many among the earlier christians were convinced that the second coming of Jesus would occur very soon. Jesus' cryptic saying: 'Some of those standing here will not taste death before they have seen the kingdom of God come in power' (Mk 9, 1) was interpreted as implying that the end of the world would come within a few years. From what Paul wrote to the Thessalonians in 51 A.D. we know that he expected that he himself and most of his christians would be alive when Christ was to come (1 Thess 4, 15). The same is implied in his letter to the Corinthians of 57 A.D. (1 Cor 15, 51). The early christians were so time-conscious about the final salvation which Jesus' second coming would bring that Paul could write: 'Salvation is nearer now than when you first believed' (Rom 13, 11).

It is not difficult to see that such high-strung expectations had undesirable consequences for the christian's life. Some new converts at Thessalonica had stopped working altogether and were idly waiting for the last day. Paul disapproved of this (2 Thess 2, 6) and warned against exaggerated oracles foretelling the imminence of the Lord's Day (2 Thess 2, 2). Some felt deceived and disappointed when Christ did not come as soon as they had anticipated: 'Where now is the promise of his coming?' St Peter had to answer this question at length (2 Pet 3, 3-10).

Christians whose life is dominated by the belief that the end of the universe can come any day, are no longer interested in building up their own world. They are literally like people looking up into the sky. They forget that they have a job to do on earth. Luke made it his concern to correct such a mistaken attitude. At the ascension scene he reports the remark, 'Men of Galilee, why stand there looking up into the sky? This Jesus — will come in the same way as you have seen him go' (Acts 1, 11). In other words, he will come by himself, through his own power, at his own convenient time. Don't waste your time fretting about when and how he comes. Get down to doing the job Christ expects of you.

In his Gospel, Luke frequently discredits exaggerated pre-occupation with Christ's second coming. Whenever the question of the date of Christ's coming is mentioned, Luke points to the task that has to be done first. He records that, at Jesus' entry into Jerusalem, some people thought that the kingdom of heaven would now come immediately (Lk 19, 11). Jesus counters this by giving the parable of the talents: the end will not come immediately, but the entrusted responsibility should be taken in hand at once (Lk 19, 12-27). Persecutions and upheavals, even the destruction of Jerusalem, does not mean that the end will come immediately (Lk 12,7). When the apostles inquire about the date of the last things, Jesus is reported to give a stern answer. 'It is not for you to know about dates and times.' Instead the apostles should devote their energies to bearing witness for him 'to the ends of the earth' (Acts 1, 6-8). Jesus' cryptic saying about the coming of the kingdom even during the first generation is interpreted by Luke with reference to another saying of Jesus: 'You cannot tell by observation *when* the kingdom of God comes. There will be no saying, "Look, here it is!" or "There it is!" for in fact the kingdom of God is among you' (Lk 17, 20-21).

The Church and the Spirit

Before the end of time could come, Christ wanted there to be *an era of the Church.*[77] Luke thought this so important that he devoted a whole book to it, the Acts of the Apostles. For him it was a fundamental mistake to identify christian history with the life of Jesus. Because after Jesus' redemptive work God continued to act through the Spirit. The Acts of the Apostles have rightly been called the Gospel of the Holy Spirit. For, starting from Jesus' promise of the Spirit in the first chapter and the account of Pentecost in the second, Luke shows throughout the Acts how the Holy Spirit made Jesus' followers into a world Church.

By recognising the independent role of the Church, Luke drew attention to a theological fact of paramount importance.

It was the fact that Jesus himself had not decided about everything that should be done in his Church. New and unexpected developments would take place among Jesus' followers. These new developments, too, have a divine origin. They are brought about by the Holy Spirit from within the Church. They should be accepted with equal readiness as the explicit rulings of Jesus himself. Of course, there is no contradiction between what Jesus said and did and the new directives given by the Spirit. When writing his Gospel, Luke shows that Jesus' words and actions contained a deeper dimension, a 'vision', an inner dynamism that *could* find expression in such far-reaching decisions taken by the later Church body.

Let me work out one example. Luke narrates in the Acts of the Apostles how the early Church came to accept non-Jews into their community. The baptism of the household of Cornelius was truly a new beginning here. Previously, non-Jews had only been admitted if they were Jewish proselytes who had been circumcised. Cornelius and his household were Romans who became Christians without first being made imitation-Jews by circumcision. Luke stresses that this was God's doing. Cornelius was urged by an angel to send for Peter (Acts 10, 1-8). Peter was warned through a vision not to consider anything profane that God counts clean (Acts 10, 1-16). Finally, when Peter preached the Gospel of Jesus, Cornelius and his family were filled with the Holy Spirit (Acts 10, 17-44). It was this clear manifestation of the Holy Spirit that convinced Peter most of all that pagans can become christians without an intermediate stage of circumcision (Acts 10, 45-48). Luke narrates how Peter had to justify this decision in the Jerusalem Church (Acts 11, 1-18) and how it led to the first Council of the Church which formally declared that non-Jews could be admitted to the Church without requiring them to undergo circumcision or keep Mosaic law (Acts 15, 1-12).

Admitting non-Jews without requiring circumcision was a momentous decision that had not been taken by Jesus but by the Church. It went far *beyond* what Jesus said. In a way it was a departure from Jesus' own practice. This is clear from the very discussion in the early Church, where the matter was decided not with reference to rulings of Jesus, but by a recognition of the will of the Spirit. Secondly, we know from the Gospels that Jesus restricted his own ministry explicitly to the Jews. 'Do not take the road to gentile lands, and do not enter any Samaritan town. But go rather to the lost sheep of the house of Israel' (Mt 10, 5). 'I was sent to the lost sheep of the house of Israel, and to them alone' (Mt 15, 24). We may be sure that in the discussion as to whether non-Jews could be admitted as they were (without circumcision; cf Acts 15, 1), some of the Jewish christians will have quoted these sayings of Jesus. Their narrow interpretation of Jesus' words will have stressed the need of first becoming a Jew, before being able to benefit from Jesus' redemption. It was necessary therefore for the Early Christians to become somewhat detached from a too literal adherence to Jesus' words. They had to learn that to understand Jesus' mind we should not limit ourselves to his external sayings and deeds alone. We should grasp above all the prophetic dimension in Jesus' life which went far beyond his immediate practice.

If we read the Gospel of St Luke in this light, we see how he handles this value of inner vision and prophetic dimension. Luke reflects on Jesus' attitude towards Samaritans, people considered heretics and religious outcasts by the Jews. Jesus refused to curse the Samaritan village which failed to give him accommodation (Lk 10, 29-37). He said about the centurion at Capernaum, 'I tell you, nowhere, even in Israel, have I found faith like this' (Lk 7,9). In such incidents Luke rightly sees an attitude of Jesus towards non-Jews that transcends Mosaic law and that embraces a vision of the Church in which Samaritans and Romans can feel at home as much as the Jews.

Ministry and the Spirit

Stressing new forms of ministry is another of Luke's explicit aims. There is evidence to show that the question of 'apostolic' succession was not so easily solved in the early Church. The twelve apostles who had been chosen by Christ himself and who had been personally instructed by him were accorded such an exceptional respect and authority that it looked as if no one else could take their place. Yet this was essential for the continued existence and spread of the Church. However privileged a position the twelve occupied, their task had to be continued by persons who had not been directly chosen by Christ himself, who were converts themselves and who might come from a non-Jewish background.

When writing the Acts of the Apostles, Luke tackles this problem head on. In the very first chapter he narrates how Matthias was chosen to replace Judas. 'He was assigned a place among the twelve apostles' (Acts 1, 26). Complaints from the Greek-speaking christians at Jerusalem that they were being neglected led to the appointment of seven deacons (Acts 6, 1-6). Although the original purpose of this diaconate focussed more on material ministration, it is clear from the accounts of two of them — Stephen and Philip — that they were doing the same work as the apostles as far as preaching the Gospel is concerned. But they could not give the Holy Spirit by the imposition of hands. A complete breakthrough took place at Antioch when the congregation there under the guidance of the Holy Spirit laid their hands on Paul and Barnabas and sent them on a missionary tour (Acts 14, 1-3). Their official status was confirmed in the Council of Jerusalem (Acts 15, 12). This opened the way to many others being drawn into the ministry, such as Timothy from Lystra, Titus from Galatia, Apollos from Alexandria, Epaphras from Colossae, and many others.

In harmony with his technique of seeing a future vision in Jesus' actions, Luke searched the life of Jesus to find confirmation for this development in the Church. He found it in the fact that Jesus sent out more disciples than only the twelve. In his Gospel Luke makes most of this event. After reporting how Jesus sent out 'the twelve' in a rather short passage (Lk 9, 1-6), he recounts at length how Jesus sent out 'seventy-two others' who are given the same instructions as the apostles (Lk 10, 1-24). Just as twelve stands for the twelve tribes of Israel, so seventy-two denotes all the nations of the earth according to the Jewish symbolism of the time. It is to the seventy-two disciples that Jesus says 'Whoever listens to you listens to me; whoever rejects you rejects me' (Lk 10,16). It is very likely that the sending out of the 'other' disciples was a relatively minor occurrence in the life of Jesus. It was probably almost forgotten and certainly overshadowed by the special attention Jesus lavished on the twelve. But for St Luke this small incident had prophetic value as it pointed to what was to happen in the later Church. It was not against the mind of Jesus that the work of the twelve was to be taken over by the seventy-two of all the nations.

Focus on women in Luke's Gospel

All four Gospels affirm that women played a special part in Jesus' life. It was noted particularly in Luke's Gospel. Luke records episodes not found in the other Gospel accounts. He introduces Elizabeth (Lk 1, 5-45), the prophetess Anna (Lk 2, 36-38), the widow of Naim (Lk7, 11-17), the women who ministered unto Jesus (Lk 8, 1-3), the woman who was bent over (Lk 13, 38-42) and the weeping women of Jerusalem (Lk 23, 27-31). Luke preserved two special parables involving women: the housewife who lost a drachma (Lk 15, 8-10) and the tenacious widow (Lk 18, 1-8). Women also mentioned in the other Gospels, receive special focus with Luke: Mary Magdalene (Lk 7, 36-50), Mary and Martha (Lk 10, 38-42) and the poor widow who offered two coins in the temple (Lk 21, 1-4). Jesus' relationship to women is an outspoken theme of this Gospel.

Why did Luke focus attention on the role played by women in Jesus' life? Obviously here, as in the other cases,

Luke acted in response to a need in the early Church. In many communities women played a leading role. Apollos' conversion at Ephesus was as much due to Priscilla as to Aquila (Acts 18, 18-26). In Corinth it was Chloë who sent messengers to Paul to inform him about problems in the Church (1 Cor 1, 11). The community of Cenchreae had a lady deacon, 'Phoebe our fellow-christian' (Rom 16, 1-2). At Philippi, where Luke worked a long time in the apostolate, we find mention of three prominent ladies: Lydia, who ran a prosperous business in purple dresses and in whose house the local community met (Acts 16, 14-15); Euodia and Syntyche about whom Paul could say 'these women who shared my struggles in the cause of the Gospel' (Phil 4, 2-3). It is obvious that these women and others whose names have not been recorded, were concerned about their own specific role in the christian community.

When recalling incidents of Jesus' life involving women, Luke has a very rich message to give. In his view women are equal recipients of Jesus' grace. Like men, women too should be converted (Mary Magdalene), listen to Jesus' word (Mary and Martha), pray with perseverance (the tenacious widow), and share in his sufferings and cross (Lk 23, 49). The role of being a mother, with its sorrows and joys, is reflected on in persons such as the widow of Naim, Elizabeth and Our Lady. Jesus takes examples from women's everyday tasks: drawing water from the well, grinding corn with the millstones, sweeping the house, mixing leaven through the dough, and preparing food for guests. Jesus had observed such activities and invested some of them with profound symbolic meaning. In these and many other ways Luke's passages on women yield an unexpectedly rich treasury of pointers and reflections.

Did St Luke however advert to the *ministry* of women? Did he, in presenting these words and deeds of Jesus, want to reflect on women's involvement *in the apostolate?* Does St Luke's Gospel contain a 'vision' of how women could be given a more responsible role within the christian community?

It is in the light of this question that certain other passages in Luke's Gospel receive a profound significance. Luke narrates how women too accompanied Jesus in his apostolic mission.

> 'Jesus went journeying from town to town and village to village, proclaiming the good news of the kingdom of God. With him were the Twelve and a number of women who had been set free from evil spirits and infirmities: Mary, known as Mary of Magdala, from whom seven devils had come out, Joanna, the wife of Chusa, a steward of Herod's, Susanna, and many others. These women provided for them out of their own resources' (Lk 8, 1-3).

Luke realised that, given the social status of women in those days, it was impossible for Jesus to draw them into the apostolic team. In the early Church as Luke knew it, a truly equal partnership of women in the ministry was also excluded, on sociological grounds. But it is certain that Luke, who is the only evangelist to recount this aspect of Jesus' ministry, records the above incident because he saw it *had* prophetic value. If women were so closely associated with Jesus on his apostolic tours, this would certainly imply for Luke the possibility of a much greater participation of women in the era of the Church. If ever the Church were to call on a woman to take up the full ministry of a Barnabas or a Paul, Luke would not have been surprised. He would have seen an anticipation of this new development in the small band of women who shared all they had with Jesus and his apostles.

And what about Anna, the prophetess? Again, Luke is the only evangelist to make mention of her. According to his description, she was a very mature person who lived alone as a widow 'to the age of eighty-four.' Through this number, seven times twelve, she represents completeness in the faith, a christian come of age. She is a person totally dedicated to God. 'She never left the temple, but worshipped day and night, fasting and praying.' Having met Jesus, she becomes a witness to him. 'She talked about the child to all who were looking for the liberation of Jerusalem' (Lk 2, 36-38).

Why did Luke present this picture of Anna, the mature and dedicated woman, the prophetess who preached about Jesus? Is it not once more because in her he saw a vision of things to come? In the witness of this woman Luke foresaw an apostolic task meant for women that could not be realised as yet in his own times. But isn't this what inspiration is about? Wasn't this exactly Luke's constant preoccupation, namely, to show that not all decisions had been taken in Jesus' life, that completely new developments were possible under the guidance of the Holy Spirit?

This brings us to the role Our Lady plays in Luke's Gospel. As soon as Mary heard of her own election to be the mother of the 'Son of God,' she also received a commission. She was told by Gabriel that Elizabeth had conceived (Lk 1, 35-36). Mary set out on her mission. Entering Zechariah's house, she greeted Elizabeth. 'When Elizabeth heard Mary's greeting, the baby stirred in her womb. Then Elizabeth was filled with the Holy Spirit' (Lk 1, 41).

Bringing the Holy Spirit was unmistakably an apostolic prerogative. When the deacon Philip preached in Samaria, he could baptise. He could not give the Spirit. Peter and John had to come from Jerusalem to impart the Holy Spirit by the imposition of hands (Acts 8, 14-17). The converts in Ephesus lacked the Holy Spirit until Paul came and imposed hands on them (Acts 19, 6). Sometimes it was enough for the apostle to enter a house and speak the word of the Lord: as when Peter entered Cornelius's house and preached about Jesus. 'Peter was still speaking when the Holy Spirit came upon all who were listening to the message' (Acts 10, 44). This was that baptism of the Holy Spirit that the Early Christians were so conscious of. Jesus himself had said at his ascension, 'Wait for the promise made by my Father, about which you have heard me speak: John, as you know, baptised with water, but you will be baptised with the Holy Spirit' (Acts 1, 4-5). It was the distinctive sign of Jesus' own ministry. In the words of John the Baptist, 'I baptise you with water . . . He will baptise you with the Holy Spirit and with fire' (Lk 3, 16).

Our Lady's Apostolate

Baptising with the Holy Spirit was the work of the apostles. Our Lady was sent to Elizabeth to give her future son this baptism. 'I tell you, when your greeting sounded in my ears, the baby in my womb leapt for joy' (Lk 1, 44). It fulfilled the prophecy made to Zechariah by the angel, 'Your wife Elizabeth will bear a son . . . From his very birth he will be filled with the Holy Spirit' (Lk 1, 15). Of course Mary, too, had conceived and carried Jesus in her womb. But it was Mary's mediation, her coming, her voice, her person that brought this grace of the Holy Spirit. Elizabeth's response recognises this saving presence of Mary. 'Who am I that the mother of my Lord should visit me?' (Lk 1, 43). Mary too reflects on her own role when she says:

> 'So tenderly has he looked upon his servant,
> > humble as she is,
> For, from this day forth,
> all generations will count me blessed,
> so wonderfully has he dealt with me,
> > the Lord, the Mighty One.' (Lk 1, 48-49).

Traditional Catholic belief has rightly dwelt on the exalted position of Mary as the Mother of Christ. It has stressed Mary's role in redemption, her share in the dispensation of grace. Has it thereby not acknowledged in Mary the heart of the priestly function? Vatican II states:

> 'She conceived, brought forth and nourished Christ. She presented him to the Father in the Temple. She shared her Son's sufferings as he died on the cross.

86

Thus, in a wholly singular way she co-operated by her obedience, faith, hope and burning charity in the work of the Saviour in restoring supernatural life to souls. For this reason she is a mother to us in the order of grace.'[78]

Was there ever a priest so near to Christ's sacrifice as Mary was? And as to her prophetic role:

'The Mother of God joyfully showed her firstborn son to the shepherds and the Magi. . . . At the marriage feast of Cana, moved with pity, she brought about by her intercession the beginning of the miracles of Jesus as Messiah. . . .'[79]

In fact, through her charismatic intercession at Cana Mary mediates in bringing about a eucharistic symbol: the changing of water into wine. . . .

I know that Our Lady did not in fact exercise the priestly functions Christ enjoined on his apostles. She did not preside at the eucharistic table to break the bread. She did not travel round to preach, baptise and impose hands. In the social climate of those times, such functions were performed by men, not by women. As Christ accepted this social fact, so did Mary. But is it not all the more remarkable that the evangelists, and especially Luke, dwell on Mary's prominent role and praise her more than any man? Did Luke with his vision of new things to come in the Church, not deliberately draw attention to Mary to give courage to women? When Mary sings the Magnificat, does she not do so also as a woman and in the name of all women? When she speaks of the arrogant of heart and mind, the imperial powers on their thrones, and the rich who will be sent away empty-handed, could there not be some reference to male arrogance, dominance and self-sufficiency? When she speaks of the marvellous way in which God lifts up the humble and satisfies the hungry, does she not also think of how a woman, looked down upon by men, is given a key position by God?

Don't we have here an echo of the song of Deborah who foretold Barak that not he, but a woman, would have the glory of victory:

> 'Most blessed of women be Jael, the wife of Heber the Kenite, of tent-dwelling women most blessed. He asked water and she gave him milk, she brought him curds in a lordly bowl. She put her hand to the tent peg and her right hand to the workmen's mallet; she struck Sisera a blow, she crushed his head.' (Judg 5, 24-26).

Isn't Mary the 'woman' of whom it had been said:

> 'I will put enmity between you and the woman, and between your seed and her seed' (Gen 3, 15)?

It would not be right to make Mary a protagonist in the contemporary struggle for emancipation. But it seems theologically sound to say that Mary's personality and her role in redemption established once and for all the complete equality of women in God's eyes and, therefore, by right in the Church. This would naturally include, to my mind, the capability of acting in the name of Christ at the eucharist table or in the confessional. Mary's internal share in Christ's priesthood to such an eminent degree argues *a fortiori* to woman's capability of exercising external priestly functions. Luke's interest in the ministry of women makes his description of Our Lady's petition a scriptural source of hope, reflection and expectation of great possibilities.

Conclusion

As I announced at the beginning of this chapter, these last pages have gone beyond the limits of rigid scriptural argumentation. My reflections were based on Scripture, I believe, and may have captured something of value, liable to be lost in logical debate. God sometimes says more in Scripture by suggestions, hints and pointers than by flat statements. Scripture too has its dimension of vision, unavoidably vague as it deals with the future.

I have written these reflections for what they are worth, well aware that they may easily be treated with scorn by those who don't share the vision.

I should like to emphasise once more that the burden of my argument lies elsewhere. The question: Did Christ rule out women priests? I have answered in the negative. The fact that Christ chose only men to function on his apostolic team was not determined by his own specific preference, but by the social pressure of his time. In the circumstances Christ *could* not have appointed women to a priestly task. But in no way did he at any time *rule out* the possibility of women being ordained priests. On the contrary, the priesthood he instituted is of such a nature that it breaks with all previously established human limits.

Whether and when women will be admitted to sacred orders will depend on the Church. I for one am confident that guided by the Holy Spirit the Church will soon take some bold steps in this direction. Ours is not a time of a theological discussion slowed down by the cost of parchment or the pace of mules. Once awakened to the problem, the Church of today will not need centuries to assess her stand and change her practice. Those christian women who feel rightly injured by a bias in traditional theology should not lose courage. The Spirit is blowing. No power on earth can stop him.

NOTES

1. First Vatican Council, *Constitutio de Fide Catholica*, ch. 4, in *Enchiridion Symbolorum*, ed. H. DENZINGER, Freibourg, Herder, 1955 (30 ed.), no. 1795-1800.

2. *Vatican Council II*, Ed. A. FLANNERY, Dublin 1975, pg 379.

3. F.A. SULLIVAN, *De Ecclesia*, vol. I, Rome 1963, pgs 355-357.

4. 'Decree on the Means of Social Communication,' no. 8; *Vatican Council II*, l.c. pg 286; see also the Pastoral Instruction of 29 January 1971, in which the same idea is elaborated, especially no. 26, pg 303; no. 125, pg 333.

5. 'Church in the Modern World,' no. 62; ib. pg 968.

6. K. RAHNER, 'Magisterium' in *Sacramental Mundi*, ed. K. RAHNER, London 1969, vol. III, pg 357.

7. K. RAHNER. ib.

8. 'Renewal of Religious Life,' no. 14; *Vatican Council II*, o.c. pg 619.

9. 'Decree on Ecumenism,' no. 6; *Vatican Council II*, o.c. pg 459.

10. Published in Latin in *L'Osservatore Romano* 2 October 1966; English after *Christ to the World* 12 (1967) pgs 97-103; here pg 101.

11. G. BAUM, 'The Magisterium in a Changing Church,' *Concilium* 1 (1967) no. 3, pgs 34-42; here pg 42.

12. 'Decretum de Authentia Textus I Jo 5, 7,' *Acta Sanctae Sedis* 29 (1896-1897) pg 637.

13. E. MANGENOT, *Dictionnaire de la Bible*, vol.III, Paris 1898, col. 1197. M. HETZENAUER, *Novum Testamentum Greaco-Latinum*, Innsbruck 1898, vol.II, pg. 387.

14. For a classical discussion of the verse, see e.g. SIMON-DORADO, *Praelectiones ad Usum Scholarum*, Novum Testamentum, vol II, Madrid 1952, pgs 440-442.

It is worth recording that the same arguments now generally accepted had already been published by Catholic scholars before the Holy Office issued the Decree. Cf. R. CORNELY, *Historica et Critica Introductio in Utriusque Testamenti Libros Sacros*, vol III, Paris 1886, pgs 668-681.

15. A. LOISY, *Memoires pour servir à l'Histoire religieuse de notre Temps*, vol I, Paris 1930, pg 437 (translation my own).

16. Letter to Wilfred Ward, published in the *Guardian* of 9th June 1897.

17. Notable were: A. BLUDEAU who wrote articles in *Der Katholik* (1902-04) and in *Biblische Zeitschrift* (in 1903 and 1915); K. KUNSTLE, *Das Comma Johanneum auf seine Herkunft untersucht*, Freibourg 1905.

18. 'The Decree had been issued to bring to order the audacity of some private scholars who seemed to presume to have the right either to reject the authenticity of the comma joannaeum or at least to call it into doubt. The Decree had not in the least the aim to forbid that Catholic writers should study the question further ...' 2 June 1927. *Enchiridion Biblicum*, Naples 1956, ed. 3, no. 136 (121).

19. Much more information on the whole background for the decision is given by S. LYONNET in 'Le verset des Trois témoins célestes en 1 Jean 5, 7 et les décisions du Saint-Office,' Rome 1963 (manuscript, unpublished as far as I know).

20. J. KAHL, 'The Church as Slave-owner,' in *The Misery of Christianity*, Penguin 1971, pgs 28-33 (transl. from the German *Das Elend des Christentums*, Hamburg 1968).

21. LEANDER, *Quaestiones Morales Theologicae*, Lyons 1668-1692, Tome VIII, De Quarto Decalogi Praecepto, Tract. IV, Disp. I, Q. 3.

22. BARTHOLOMEW DE LAS CASAS, *Discourse against Juan Queredo, Bishop of Darien*, 1519, in L. HANKE, *Aristotle and the American Indians*, New York 1959, pg 17.

23. A good survey of the whole question is given by J. F. MAXWELL, 'The Development of Catholic Doctrine concerning Slavery,' *World Justice* 11 (1969-70) pgs 147-192; 291-324. He notes that even throughout the 18th and 19th centuries the majority of 'approved' moralists continued to support slavery with the traditional theological arguments.

24. Ed. A. FLANNERY, *Vatican Council II*, Dublin 1975, pg 930.

25. 'Declaration on the Question of the Admission of Women to the Ministerial Priesthood,' *Acta Apostolicae Sedis* 55 (1963) pgs 267-268; *Briefing* 7 (1977) no. 5 and 6.

26. The substance of this chapter was already published by me as a research paper; cf J. N. M. WIJNGAARDS, 'The Ministry of Women and Social Myth,' in *Ministries in the Church in India*, Ed. D. S. AMALORPAVADASS, New Delhi 1976, pgs 221-250.

27. F. J. J. BUYTENDIJK, *De Vrouw*, Utrecht 1961, pg 81 ff; 162-64.

28. R. SCHEIFLER, Zur Psychologie der Geschlechter, Spielinteressen des Schulalters, *Z.f.Ang. Psych.* 8 (1914), pgs 124-44;
    F. HATTWICK, Sex Differences in Behaviour of nursery school children, *Child Development* 8 (1937) pgs 343-55;
    J. CUMMINGS, The incidence of emotional symptoms in school children, *Brit. Journ. Psych.* 14 (1944) 1, pgs 151-61;
    N. G. BLURTON-JONES, An Ethological Study of some aspects of social Behaviour of Children in Nursery Schools, in *Primate Ethology*, ed. D. MORRIS, London, Weidenfeld Nicholson, 1967.

29. I. DE VORE, *Primate Behaviour*, New York:Holt Rinehart & Winston 1965.

30. W. C. YOUNG, R. W. GOY and C. H. PHOENIX, Hormones and Sexual Behaviour, *Science* 13 (1964) 212-218;
    D. A. HAMBURG and D. T. LURDE, Sex Hormones in the Development of Sex Differences in Human Behaviour, in *The Development of Sex Differences*, ed. E. E. MACCOBY, Tavistock, London 1967.

31. G. W. HARRIS and S. LEVINE, Sexual Differentiation of the Brain and its Experimental Control, *J. Phys.* 181 (1965) 379-400.

32. L. TIGER and R. FOX, *The Imperial Animal*, St Albans 1974, pg 136.

33. R. G. D'ANDRADE, Sex Differences and Cultural Institutions, in *The Development of Sex Differences*, ed. E. E. MACCOBY, Tavistock London 1967, pgs 174-204.

34. M. E. SPIRO, *Kibbutz: Venture in Utopia*, Harvard Univ. Press 1956;
L. TIGER and J. SHEPHER, *Women in the Kibbutz*, Harcourt Brace Jovanowich 1975.

35. M. F. ASHLEY-MONTAGUE, Ignorance of physiological paternity in secular knowledge and orthodox belief of the Australian aboriginees, *Oceania* 12 (1940-42), pgs 72-78. M. ELIADE, *Traité d'Histoire des Réligions*, Payot, Paris 1959, pgs 221-31.

36. H. KUHN, *De Kunst van het Oude Europa*, Pictura, Utrecht 1959, pgs 20-22; 31-33; 50, 58.

37. R. G. D'ANDRADE, Sex Differences and Cultural Institutions, ibid. (see note 33), pgs 182-85.

38. For the urban revolution, see the excellent description in V. GORDON CHILDE, *Man Makes Himself*, Mentor, New York 1951, pgs 114-42.

39. R. G. D'ANDRADE, Sex Differences and Cultural Institutions, ibid. (see note 33), pgs 174-204.

40. M. ELIADE, *Traité*, etc. (see note 35), ibid. pgs 47 ff.

41. C. S. FORD and F. BEACH, *Patterns of Sexual Behaviour*, Harper and Row, New York 1951, pgs 103, 110, 123, etc.

42. W. N. STEPHENS, *The Family in Cross-cultural Perspective*, Holt, Rinehart and Winston, 1963, pgs 256-58.

43. Good background reading to the various implications of the term 'myth' used in this sense is provided by P. MARANDA (Ed), *Mythology. Selected Readings*, Penguin 1972.

44. L. KOHLBERG, A Cognitive-Developmental Analysis of Children's Sex-Role Concepts and Attitudes, in *The Development of Sex Differences*, ed. E. E. MACCOBY, Tavistock London 1967.

45. H. BARRY, M. K. BACON and I. I. CHILD, A cross-cultural survey of some sex differences in socialization, *J. abnorm. so. psychol.* 55 (1967), 837-853.

46. This is the meaning of 'femina est mas occasionatus,' i.e. the female is the result of a defect in propagation; ARISTOTLE, *De Generatione Animalium*, II 3; THOMAS, *Summa Theol.* I Q 92, art II; ibid. Q 99, art 2 ad 1.

47. L. HUDSON, *Frames of Mind. Ability. Perception and Self-perception in the Arts and Sciences*; Penguin 1970, especially pgs 32-33; 46-47; 86-90.

48. G. PARCE, *Le Italiane se confessano*, Florence 1959.
F. SULTANI, *Mentalità e comportimento del maschio italiano*, Milan 1965.

49. J. T. NOONAN Jr, *Contraception: A History of its Treatment by the Catholic Theologians and Canonists*, Havard Univ. Press 1965, pgs 46-49; 76-81; 150-51.

50. R. NOWELL, Sex and Marriage, in *On Human Life*, ed. P. HARRIS, London, Burns & Oates 1968, pgs 45-71.

51. J. DELORME, 'Résurrection et Tombeau de Jésus,' in *La Résurrection du Christ et l'Exégèse Moderne*, ed. P. DE SURGY et al., Paris 1969, pgs 105-51.

52. H. C. KEE and F. W. YOUNG, *The Living World of the New Testament*, London 1960, pgs 111-12.

53. Instruction of the Holy Office, 20 June 1866. Quoted in J. F. MAXWELL, 'The Development of Catholic Doctrine Concerning Slavery,' *World Jurist* 11 (1969-70) pg 306 ff.

54. 'The Church in the Modern World,' no. 27; *Vatican Council II*, ed. A. FLANNERY, o.c., pg 928.

55. Ph. DELHAYE, 'Retrospective and prospective des ministères feminines dans l'Eglise,' Rév. Théol. de Louvain 3 (1972) pgs 55-75;
F. P. CHENDERLIN, 'Women as ordained priests? Should women be allowed to consecrate?' *Hom. and Past. Review* 72 (1972) no. 8, pgs25-32; 'Women priests — more thoughts but no second thoughts,' ib. 73(1973) no. 5, pgs 13-22;
J. GALOT, *La donna e i ministeri nella Chiesa*, Assisi 1973.

56. G. R. EVANS, 'Ordination of Women,' *Hom. and Past. Review* 73 (1972), No 1, pgs 29-32.

57. H. M. LEGRAND, 'Views on the Ordination of Women,' *Origins*, Jan. 6 1977. Reprinted in *Briefing* 7 (1977), No 6, pgs 22-35; here pg 27.

58. G. O'COLLINS, 'Ordination of Women,' *Tablet* 288 (1974) pgs 175-76; 213-15.

59. E. C. MEYER, 'Are there theological reasons why the church should not ordain women priests?' *Rev. for Religious* 34 (1975/76), pgs 957-67.

60. J. L. ACEBAL, 'El laicado feminino: Missiones y ministerios,' *Ciencia Tomista* 98 (1971), pgs 55-71.

J. J. BEGLEY-ARMBRUSTER, 'Women and Office in the Church,' *Am. Eccl. Review* 165 (1971) pgs 145-57.

R. GRYSON, *Le ministère des Femmes dans l'Eglise ancienne*, Gembloux 1972.

I. RAMING, *Der Ausschluss der Frau vom priesterlichen Amt*, Cologne 1973.

J. M. FORD, 'Biblical Material relevant to the Ordination of Women,' *Journal of Ecum. Studies* 10 (1973), pgs 669-94; synopsised in *Theology Digest* 22 (1974) pgs 23-28.

R. METZ, 'L'accession des femmes aux ministères ordonnées,' *Effort diaconal*, Jan-June (1974) pgs 21-30.

F. KLOSTERMANN, *Gemeinde Kirche der Zukunft*, Freiburg 1974, especially pgs 269-70.

J. M. AUBERT, *Antiféminisme et christianisme*, Paris 1975, esp. pgs 156-77.

61. Y. CONGAR, 'Éclaircissements sur la question des ministères,' *Maison Dieu* 103 (1970), pg 116.

62. Y. CONGAR in the preface to E. GIBSON, *Femmes et Ministères dans l'Eglise*, Paris 1971, pg 12.

63. J. DANIELOU; most recent statements quoted in *Informations Catholiques Internationales* No 400 (15 Jan 1972) pg 22; *Révue Theologique de Louvain* 3 (1972) pg 204; see also J. DANIELOU, 'Le ministère des femmes dans l'Eglise ancienne,' *Maison Dieu* (1961) pgs 70-96.

64. K. RAHNER, 'Letter to Pastor Bogdam of the Lutheran Synod of Bavaria.' *La Croix*, 20 April 1974; cited by H. M. LEGRAND, o.c. (note 57) pg 24.

H. VAN DER MEER'S book (Innsbruck 1962) was published in English as *Women Priests in the Catholic Church?* Philadelphia 1973.

65. J. F. MAXWELL, l.c. (note 53) pg 315.

66. A. COCHIN, *L'Abolition de l'Esclavage*, Paris 1861, vol II, pgs 442-43; quoted in J. F. MAXWELL, l.c. pg 305.

67. CORNELIUS A LAPIDE, *Commentaria in Scripturam Sacram* (Antwerp 1616) Paris 1868, vol 18, pgs 353, 396. Cf V. E. HANNON, *The Question of Women and the Priesthood*, London 1967, pgs 26-31.

68. *Briefing* 7 (1977) No 6, pg 9.

69. Quoted by H. VAN DER MEER, *Priestertum der Frau?*, Freibourg 1969, pg 150.

70. THOMAS AQUINAS, *Summa Theologica*, III Suppl., Q. 39, art 1; English transl. Burns and Oates, London 1922, vol Third Part Q. 34-68, pg 52.

71. 'Dogmatic Constitution on the Church,' No 10; *Vatican Council II*, ib. pg 361.

72. 'Dogmatic Constitution on the Church,' No 30; ib. pg 389.

73. BONAVENTURE, *Quartum Librum Sententiarum* dist. 25, a. 2, qu. 1; *Omnia Opera*, ed. Quaracchi 1889, vol IV, pgs 649-55. Cf V. E. HANNON, o.c. (note 67), pg 37.

74. Cf note 46.

75. Cf note 70.

76. J. M. FORD, o.c. (note 60) *Theology Digest* 22 (1974) pg 27.

77. For a good background study of this theme of Luke's, see H. CONZELMANN, *The Theology of Saint Luke*, Faber and Faber 1960 (from the German of 1953).

78. Dogmatic Constitution of the Church, No 61; Ed. A. FLANNERY (see note 2), pg 418.

79. Dogmatic on the Church, No 57-58; ib. pgs 416-417.